YOU CAN
play guitar

by Peter Pickow

Order No. AM 932305
US International Standard Book Number: 0.8256.1512.7
UK International Standard Book Number: 0.7119.5210.8

Exclusive Distributors:
Music Sales Corporation
257 Park Avenue South, New York, NY 10010 USA
Music Sales Limited
8/9 Frith Street, London W1V 5TZ England
Music Sales Pty. Limited
120 Rothschild Street, Rosebery, Sydney, NSW 2018, Australia

Printed and bound in the United States of America by
Vicks Lithograph and Printing

Amsco Publications
New York • London • Paris • Sydney

Compact Disc Track Listing

track	page	
1	3	**Introduction**
2	6	**How to Tune Your Guitar**
3	8	**Reading Music and Tablature**
4	11	**Playing a Melody**
5	12	*Jingle Bells*
6	14	*Ode to Joy*
7	16	*Boogie/Rock Bassline*
8	17	**Playing Chords/**The A Chord
9	18	The E7 Chord
10	19	*Tom Dooley* with simple strums
11	20	*Tom Dooley* with bass-chord strums
12		*Clementine* with bass-chord-chord strums
13	21	The D Chord/Pivot Fingers
14	22	*Old Joe Clark* with alternating bass-chord strums
15	23	*Simple Gifts*
16	24	The Flick
17		*Old Joe Clark*
18	25	Waltz Time Strums
19		*Drink to Me Only With Thine Eyes*
20	26	**The Key of D Major/**The A7 Chord
21	27	Pivot Practice in D Major
22		Syncopation
23	28	*Sloop John B*
24	29	The E7 Chord as II7
25	30	*My Bonnie*
26	31	**Playing Lead Guitar/**The Blues Scale
27	32	*Good Morning Blues*
28	34	**Minor Chords/**The A Minor Chord
29		The D Minor Chord
30	35	*Johnny Has Gone For a Soldier*
31	36	**Suspended Chords/**The Dsus4 Chord
32	37	The Gsus4 Chord
33	38	The A7sus4 Chord
34		*Silent Night*
35	40	**Playing Broken-Chord Accompaniment/**Picks and Fingers
36	41	*Johnny Has Gone for a Soldier*
37		Broken Chords in Waltz Time
38	42	*Silent Night*
39	44	**The Key of G Major**
40	46	*Amazing Grace*
41	47	**The Key of C Major/**The F Chord
42	48	*Oh, Susanna*
43	49	**Playing Fingerstyle/**"Dead Thumb" Picking
44		Hammerons
45	50	The B7 Chord
46	51	Slides
47	52	*Sugar Babe*
48	55	*Railroad Bill*
49	57	**Developing Your Repertoire/**The Blues
50	59	*Frankie and Johnny*
51	60	Memphis shuffle exercise
52	61	*C.C. Rider*
53	63	Rock/power chords
54	64	*La Bamba*
55	66	exercises for "Crossroads"
56	70	*Crossroads*
57	73	Pop/new chords for "Morning Has Broken"
58	74	*Morning Has Broken*
59	77	exercises for "Aura Lee"
60	79	*Aura Lee*
61	81	Ragtime and Jazz/ *The Entertainer*
62	84	exercises for "A-Tisket A-Tasket"
63	85	*A-Tisket A-Tasket*
64	86	*Estudio*
65	89	*Romanze*

Table of Contents

Introduction   3
Your Guitar   4
Holding Your Guitar   5
How to Tune Your Guitar   6
   Relative Tuning   6
   Tuning to a Piano   7
Reading Music and Tablature   8
   Fretting   8
   Reading Rhythms   9
Playing a Melody   11
   Picks and Fingers   11
   Eighth Notes   11
     Jingle Bells   12
     Ode to Joy   14
Playing a Bassline   15
   Rests and Ties   15
     Boogie/Rock Bassline   16
Playing Chords   17
   The A Chord   17
   Strumming   17
   The E7 Chord   18
     Tom Dooley   19
   The Bass-Chord Strum   19
     Tom Dooley   20
   The Bass-Chord-Chord Strum   20
     Clementine   20
   The D Chord   21
   Pivot Fingers   21
   The Alternating Bass-Chord Strum   22
     Old Joe Clark   22
   Pivot Practice in A Major   23
     Simple Gifts   23
   The Flick   24
     Old Joe Clark   24
   Waltz Time Strums   25
     Drink to Me Only With Thine Eyes   25
The Key of D Major   26
   The A7 Chord   26
   The G Chord   26
   Pivot Practice in D Major   27
   Syncopation   27
     Sloop John B.   28
   The E7 Chord as II7   29
     My Bonnie   30
Playing Lead Guitar   31
   The Blues Scale   31
     Good Morning Blues   32
Minor Chords   34
   The A Minor Chord   34
   The D Minor Chord   34

Chord Practice in A Minor   35
     Johnny Has Gone for a Soldier   35
Suspended Chords   36
   The Dsus 4 Chord   36
   The Gsus 4 Chord   37
   The A7sus4 Chord   38
   Suspended Chord Practice   38
     Silent Night   38
Playing Broken-Chord Accompaniment   40
   Picks and Fingers   40
     Johnny Has Gone for a Soldier   41
   Broken Chords in Waltz Time   41
     Silent Night   42
The Key of G Major   44
   The G7 Chord   44
   The C Chord   44
   The D7 Chord   44
   Chord Practice in G Major   45
     Amazing Grace   46
The Key of C Major   47
   The F Chord   47
     Oh, Susanna   48
Playing Fingerstyle   49
   "Dead Thumb" Picking   49
   Hammerons   49
   The B7 Chord   50
   Slides   51
     Sugar Babe   52
   Pattern Picking   54
     Railroad Bill   55
Developing Your Repertoire   57
   The Blues   57
     Frankie and Johnny   59
     C.C. Rider   61
   Rock   63
     La Bamba   64
     Crossroads   70
   Pop   73
     Morning Has Broken   74
     Aura Lee (Love Me Tender)   79
   Ragtime and Jazz   81
     The Entertainer   82
     A-Tisket A-Tasket   85
   Classical   86
     Estudio   87
     Romanze   89
Further Study   91
Table of Notes   91
Table of Chords   92

Introduction

It's true. With a little study and practice, anyone can play guitar—and this proven guitar program will give you the chance to play a variety of popular styles—including rock, pop, blues, jazz, ragtime, and classical music. This easy, step-by-step method will guide you through all the basics of guitar performance and technique. You'll strengthen and develop these important playing skills in exciting performance sessions when you play the popular hits of Elvis Presley, the Beach Boys, Cream, the Animals—as well as memorable tunes recorded by James Taylor, Judy Collins, Cat Stevens, Ella Fitzgerald, Robert Johnson, Ritchie Valens, and Los Lobos.

This comprehensive guitar method is easy and fun—and does not rely on tricks and shortcuts that only work for certain songs in certain keys. On the contrary, you can learn to play a variety of guitar music in different keys—and develop all the skills you need to learn hundreds of new songs on your own after you finish the program.

Whether you intend to be a professional guitar player or songwriter, or simply wish to play for your community, family, and friends—this book is for you. So, get ready to learn the basics of guitar as you play the world's most popular songs.

Your Guitar

This book is designed to be used with any six-string guitar—acoustic or electric. If you are using an acoustic guitar, it will either be a *nylon-string* or a *steel-string* guitar. On nylon-string guitars, the top (higher pitched) three strings are made of nylon and the bottom (lower pitched) three are wound with steel. On a steel-string guitar, all six strings are made of metal. The top two or three strings are plain metal—and the bottom three or four strings are metal wound. Electric guitars always have steel strings. In general, the easiest type of guitar for a beginner to play is a nylon-string, but you can use any type of guitar to learn the techniques, concepts, and songs in this book. If you are left-handed, you may want to consider getting a left-handed guitar. If you use a left-handed guitar for this program, simply reverse the left- and right-hand instructions.

Acoustic and electric guitars exhibit other small differences. These include the type of bridge and tuning pegs, the presence or absence of a whammy bar, the shape of the body, and so on. Here is a diagram to help you learn the names of the parts of your guitar.

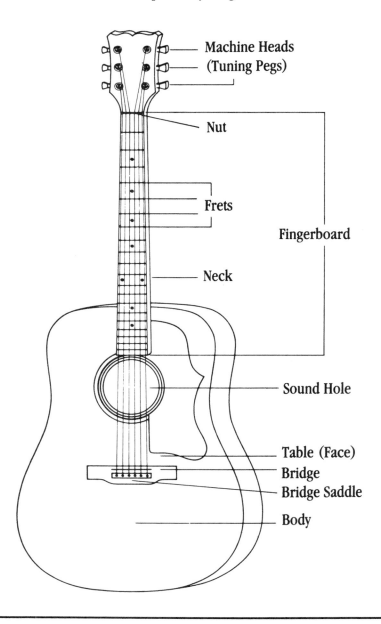

Holding Your Guitar

You probably will do most of your practicing sitting down. Place the guitar on your right thigh. Hold it against your body and let your right forearm rest comfortably on top. Your right elbow should be fairly close to your body.

You will need a strap to play in a standing position. If you don't already have a strap, you can get one at any music store. Be sure to tell the salesperson what kind of guitar you have so that you will be sure to get a strap that is right for you.

Attach the strap to the guitar and place it over your left shoulder. While sitting and holding the guitar in your usual position, adjust the strap until it is just taut. When you stand up, the strap will hold the guitar in the proper position.

How to Tune Your Guitar

Before you begin to practice or play, you should always make sure that your guitar is in tune. You tune each string to its correct pitch by turning the appropriate *tuning peg*.

Relative Tuning

If your guitar is already pretty well in tune, you can use the *relative tuning* method to tune up.

- Use a left-hand finger to press down on the sixth string (low E) just behind (to the left of) the fifth fret. When you pluck this string, you will hear an A note. This note should sound the same as the fifth string played *open* (that is, without being fretted by a left-hand finger).
- If the fifth string (or A string) does not sound in tune, use the tuning peg to loosen it until it sounds lower than the sixth string, fifth fret. Then slowly bring it up to pitch.
- When your A string is in tune, fret it at the fifth fret. This note is D, and should sound the same as the open D, or fourth, string.
- When your D string is in tune, fret it at the fifth fret. This note is G, and should sound the same as the open G, or third, string.
- When your G string is in tune, fret it at the fourth fret. This note is B, and should sound the same as the open B, or second, string.
- When your B string is in tune, fret it at the fifth fret. This note is E, and should sound the same as the open high E, or first, string.

  This diagram summarizes the relative tuning method.

Relative Tuning Method

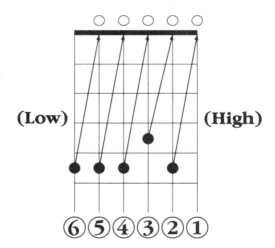

(Low)   (High)

⑥⑤④③②①

Tuning to a Piano

You can use a tuned piano or electronic keyboard instrument to tune each string of your guitar. Here are the notes on the keyboard that correspond to the open strings of the guitar. These notes represent the actual sounds of the guitar strings. However, music for guitar is written one octave higher than it sounds to make it easier to read.

Tuning to a Piano

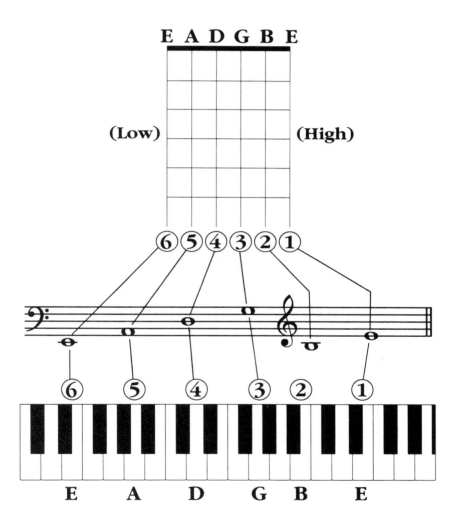

Reading Music and Tablature

The song melodies in this book are written in standard music notation. You can use the "Table of Notes" toward the end of the book to play the melody to any of the songs that may be unfamiliar to you. The accompaniment parts are written in special notation that will make it easy for you to start playing terrific parts right away. Many songs and examples are presented in *tablature*, a well-known system of notation designed specially for guitarists. This system has a long and venerable history dating back to the lute music of the Renaissance. Our modern tablature system uses a *staff* composed of six lines. Each line represents a string of the guitar, with string **1** being the highest, and string **6**, the lowest.

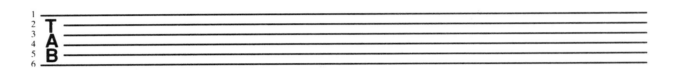

Fretting

In order to *fret* a string, your left-hand fingertip must press it to the fingerboard just behind (to the left of) a fret. Fret numbers placed on lines of guitar tablature tell you which fret to play on a given string. (Fret **1** is the one nearest to the tuning pegs.) For instance, this tab tells you to play three different notes on the low E string. Use your left middle finger to press down on the string at the second fret. Then sound this note by brushing across the string with the side of your right-hand thumb. Release your middle finger and press down on the first fret with your index finger, and play the second note. Then play the string without fretting, as indicated by the **0** for *open string*.

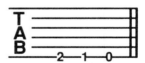

If you hear buzzing or a muffled tone when you play fretted notes, your fretting finger is probably too close to (or too far away from) the fret. Or it may be that you are just not pressing down hard enough. Here are several things to keep in mind that will help you to get a clear sound on fretted notes.

- **Use your fingertips.** Arch your fingers so that they come straight down on the strings. Imagine you are making an "okay" sign with your thumb and index finger.
- **Keep your thumb in the middle of the back of the neck.** Although it is tempting to let your thumb slide up and peek over the top of the neck, keep it in the middle, just opposite the middle finger. This will

help your fingers to stay properly arched.

• **Keep your wrist low and your elbow close to the body.** This will also help you to bring your fingers down accurately and firmly.

• **Avoid tensing your shoulder.** This bad habit will limit your mobility. If your shoulder and arm are not relaxed, it can be difficult to change fret positions smoothly.

Don't worry if fretting notes feels a little uncomfortable at first. It normal for beginners to get sore fingertips. (This is especially true if you are playing on a steel-string acoustic guitar.) As you practice, your fingertips will develop calluses, and fretting notes will begin to feel more natural to you.

Reading Rhythms

With tablature to show you where to put your fingers, you now need to know how long to hold each note. First let's look at three different types of note values and their duration in beats. Notice how the notes are distinguished by the presence or absence of a line or *stem*—and by the appearance of the *notehead,* which may be either outlined or filled in. In tablature, the notehead is replaced by a fret number, which may be plain or circled.

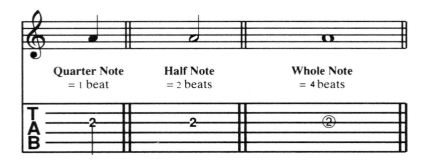

These basic note values form a pattern. The *half note* (which lasts for two beats) is twice the length of the *quarter note* (which lasts for one beat). Similarly, the *whole note* (four beats) is twice the length of the half note (two beats).

A *time signature* at the beginning of a song tells you how many beats there are per *measure* (or *bar*) and what kind of note equals one beat. The most common time signature is $\frac{4}{4}$, which is often referred to as *common time* and abbreviated as **C**. The top **4** of $\frac{4}{4}$ tells you that there are four beats in each measure. The bottom **4** means that a quarter note gets one beat.

Try playing a few bars of $\frac{4}{4}$ time with four quarter-notes per measure. You can use a metronome or just tap your foot to keep the beat even. Count out loud as you use your right thumb to play the notes slowly and evenly on the sixth and fifth strings. The double barline with two dots at the end of this piece is a *repeat sign,* which tells you to go back to the beginning and play the section over again.

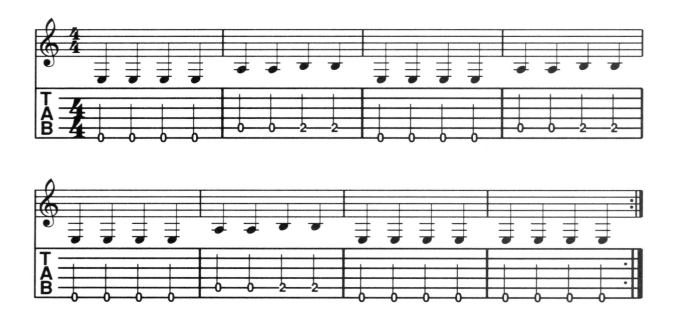

Now take a look at the first phrase of the traditional melody "Jingle Bells," which contains quarter notes, half notes, and whole notes in $\frac{4}{4}$. Count each beat aloud as you clap the rhythm of "Jingle Bells"— that is, count out each beat number slowly and evenly, but clap only on the beats that correspond to notes of the melody (these beat numbers appear in boxes).

Playing a Melody

When you play the melody to a song, or improvise a solo, you use *single-line style*. This approach is also known as *single-note style, single-string style,* or playing *lead.* To get started, let's explore some important right-hand techniques.

Picks and Fingers

There are two basic approaches to right-hand technique: fingerstyle and playing with a pick. A well-rounded guitarist is able to play in both these styles. We will start out using the right-hand index and middle fingers. Try playing the first string (high E) with first your index finger and then your middle finger. Keep these suggestions in mind as you alternate the two fingers slowly and evenly.

- **Use rest strokes.** To execute a *rest stroke,* move your finger straight across the string and let the finger come to rest on the next lower string. Rest strokes ensure evenness of attack and tone and also help your rhythm and timekeeping.
- **Keep your fingers straight.** With each stroke, your finger should move from the knuckle at the base of your finger.
- **Arch your wrist.** This helps you to keep your fingers straight.
- **Keep your fingers perpendicular to the strings.** Also extend your thumb a bit to the left to pull your hand into line.

  Now get ready to play the first phrase of "Jingle Bells" with your index and middle fingers. Start with the index finger, and then alternate as shown (*i* = index, *m* = middle). The tablature will show you the string and fret for each note. The numbers next to the notes in the standard notation tell you which left-hand fingers to use for the fretted notes (**1** = index, **2** = middle, **3** = ring, **4** = pinky). Count each beat as you play.

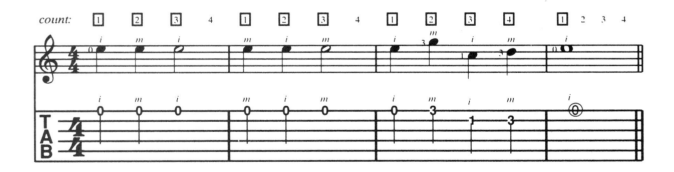

Eighth Notes

Many tunes contain short notes that are worth only one-half of a beat. These notes are called *eighth notes.*

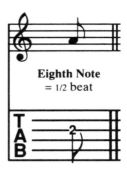

Eighth Note
= 1/2 beat

Eighth notes often occur in groups of two or more. These groups are linked with a bar called a *beam*. Count and clap the rhythm in the second phrase of "Jingle Bells." Remember to count each beat number aloud, but clap only on the beats that appear in boxes. The eighth notes in the second measure are counted with the word "and" between beats.

Now play the full chorus of "Jingle Bells," beginning on the first string. Practice "Jingle Bells" (without counting) until you can play it with confidence at a moderate speed.

Jingle Bells

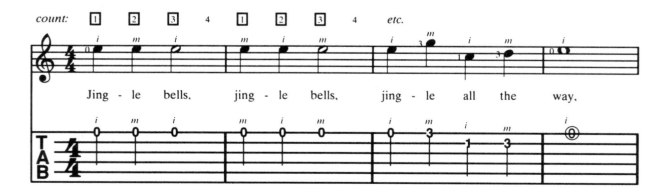

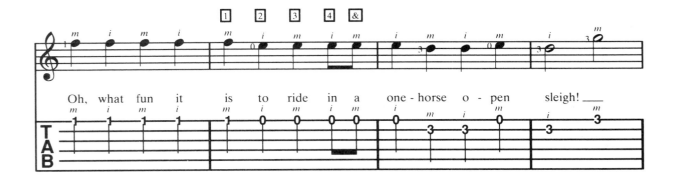

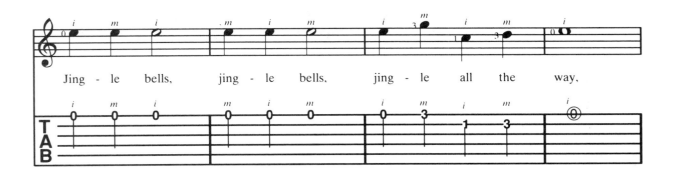

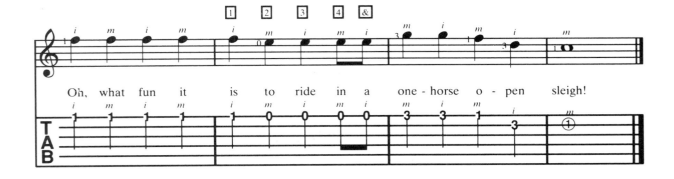

"Ode to Joy" is another good practice melody for single-line playing. Use the top three strings to play this famous theme from Beethoven's Ninth Symphony. Pay attention to the right-hand fingering indications as you skip from the third string to the first string in the twelfth measure.

Ode to Joy

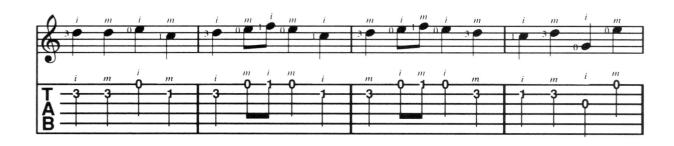

Playing a Bassline

So far, you've used the top three strings to play song melodies. These high strings are called the *treble strings.* The remaining three lower strings are referred to as the *bass strings.* These bass strings are often used to play *rhythm figures*—the powerful, driving parts that propel many rock and rhythm & blues tunes. In the next section, you'll learn a boogie/rock bassline that you can use to back up hundreds of songs.

Rests and Ties

In the last measure of the "Boogie Rock/Bassline," you will see two kinds of *rests.* The *eighth rest* (ɤ) indicates silence for one-half of a beat. The *quarter rest* (ɂ) indicates silence for one beat. To stop the low E string from ringing through the rests, *damp* it (touch it lightly) with the heel of your right hand.

Another new symbol appearing in the last measure is the curved line connecting the eighth-note E to the final quarter-note E. This curved line is called a *tie,* which indicates that you hold the note through for the combined lengths of the eighth note and quarter note—a total of one-and-a-half beats.

You may want to try playing this bassline with a pick. For acoustic or electric guitar styles, most players use a heavy or medium pick in the standard teardrop shape. Keep your hand relaxed so that the pick rests on your curled index finger while the thumb holds it in place. Allow the pick to be as flexible in your hand as possible without dropping it. One of the advantages of using a pick is that it makes it easy to play a fast string of notes with alternating *downstrokes* and *upstrokes.* The movement should come mostly from the wrist, but you can put some force behind each stroke by using your forearm a bit also. A downstroke (⊓) is down toward the floor and an upstroke (ᐯ) is up toward the ceiling.

Now try the "Boogie/Rock Bassline." If you don't want to use a pick, you can play this whole piece with your thumb. Use your left index finger (**1**) to play the notes on the second fret and your left ring finger (**3**) for the fourth-fret notes.

Boogie/Rock Bassline

Playing Chords

A *chord* is a group of three or more notes. Chords are important to guitarists because it is through a knowledge of different *chord forms* that we shape accompaniments. Basically, when you play just the chords to a song, you are playing *rhythm guitar,* as opposed to lead.

Chord diagrams, also called *chord boxes, chord windows,* or *chord frames,* make it easy to learn new chords. You will often see chord diagrams above the melody line in songbooks. A chord diagram shows you where to put your left-hand fingers on the strings of the guitar—and tells you the name of the chord you are playing.

The A Chord

The chord diagrammed below is called "A" (short for "A major") because it is the main chord in the key of A major. Saying that a song is "in the key of A" means that the notes of the melody are drawn from an A major scale—and that the A chord is the *tonic* or *I chord* (pronounced "one chord"). Use your left hand to fret this chord as shown, then strum a few times with your the backs of the fingertips of your right hand. Try to avoid hitting the low E string as indicated by the **X** in the diagram: In most cases, it's best when the A note (which is called the *root* of the chord) is the lowest note sounded.

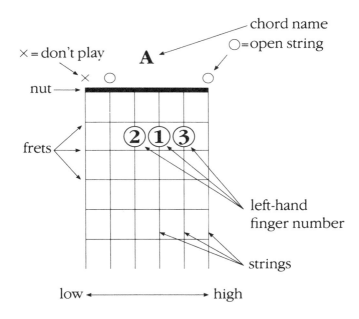

Strumming

Practice strumming in rhythm as you play the exercise below. It is probably easiest for you to use your fingers to strum—but feel free to experiment with the pick. Each of the slash marks indicates a downward strum with the time value of a quarter note (one beat). Strum slowly and evenly and count out loud. If any of the notes in the chord sound muffled or are buzzing, check your left-hand position. It is all right to play until your left hand feels tired, but stop for a rest if it starts to hurt.

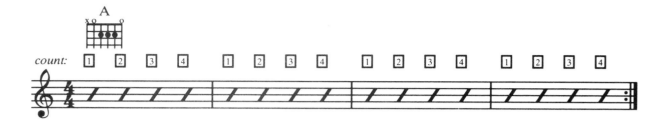

The E7 Chord

The *E7 chord* is another important chord in the key of A major. In this context, E7 is called the *V7 chord* (pronounced "five-seven") because it is built on the fifth note of the A major scale.

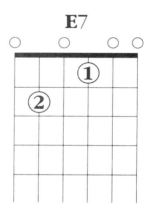

When learning any new chord, strive to bring your left-hand fingers down on the strings as a group rather than placing them one at a time. Think of the individual finger positions for each new chord as a unit or *chord shape.* With this in mind, try strumming the E7 chord a few times.

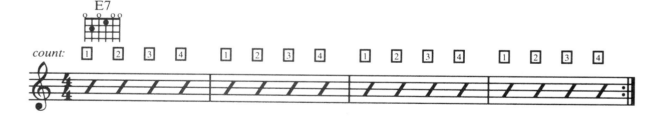

There are lots of songs that you can play using just the A and E7 chords. Let's put these chords together now in a complete song arrangement. This will give you some valuable practice in changing chords. No matter how well you know a chord, it is always a little tough at first to change smoothly to other chords and back again. To get this technique down, here are a few things to keep in mind.

• **Keep your fingers close to the strings.** Don't let your fingers fly off into space when you go to grab a new chord. The trick to changing chords quickly and smoothly is economy of movement. When you change from A to E7, just slide your first finger back one fret along the same string. Your second finger just moves over one string on the same fret.

- **Move all of your fingers at once.** This takes some practice, but will become more natural the better you know the chord positions.
- **Start changing to a new chord a little early.** In order to keep the rhythm steady, you must cheat the time value of the last strum before a chord change by a fraction. With practice, this becomes a natural reaction. Just remember that the first strum of a new chord is the most important.

Now here is "Tom Dooley," a traditional American favorite which was a gold-record hit for the Kingston Trio in 1958. Strum down across the strings once every beat, but hold the half-note strum in the last measure for two beats.

Tom Dooley

The Bass-Chord Strum
================

Let's explore how a *bass-chord strum* can really add movement to the accompaniment part to "Tom Dooley." For this strum, play a single bass note on beats one and three and strum only on beats two and four: bass-chord-bass-chord. This bass-chord strum actually gives you more time to change from one chord to the next, because the first beat of every measure is an open string. Each chord has one bass note that is considered the *primary bass*. Usually this primary bass is the root of the chord. For the A chord, use the open A string (⑤) as the primary bass—and for the E7, use the open low E string (⑥).

Now play "Tom Dooley" again using single bass notes on the fifth and sixth strings (as indicated by the circled numbers ⑤ and ⑥). Play each single bass note with your right-hand thumb (p = thumb). Then strum down across the remaining strings with your fingers. If you are using a pick, play the single bass note with a firm stroke that brings the pick to rest on the next highest string. Then lift the pick slightly before strumming down across the remaining strings.

Tom Dooley

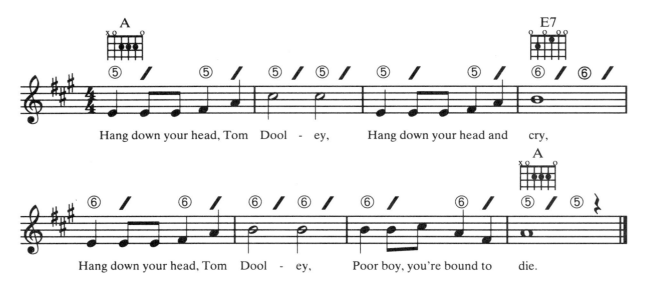

Hang down your head, Tom Dool - ey, Hang down your head and cry,

Hang down your head, Tom Dool - ey, Poor boy, you're bound to die.

The Bass-Chord-Chord Strum

The *bass-chord-chord strum* is simply a variation on the bass-chord strum you have just learned. This variation works well with songs in $\frac{3}{4}$ time (also called *waltz time*). In $\frac{3}{4}$ time, there are three quarter-notes to each measure. "Clementine" is a good example of a song in $\frac{3}{4}$ time. This song starts off with an incomplete measure, which is called a *pickup measure* (or *pickup*). Notice that the last measure has only two beats to make up for the one in the pickup. Play "Clementine" at a moderate speed.

Clementine

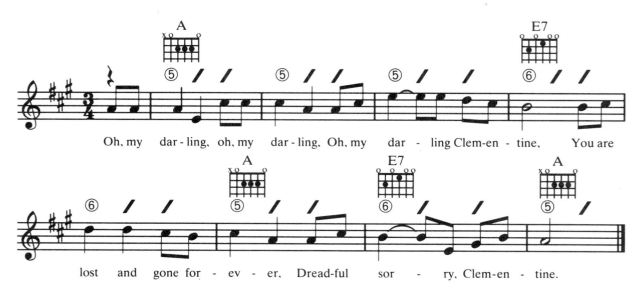

Oh, my dar - ling, oh, my dar - ling, Oh, my dar - ling Clem-en - tine, You are

lost and gone for - ev - er, Dread-ful sor - ry, Clem-en - tine.

The D Chord

The D chord is the IV chord (pronounced "four chord") in the key of A major. Once you know the D chord, you can play thousands of songs in the key of A. Try strumming it a few times, making sure not to sound the low E and A strings.

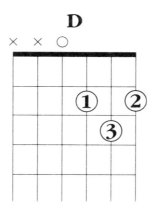

D

Pivot Fingers

An important concept that will help you to change chords smoothly is that of *pivot fingers*. A pivot finger is one that does not move when you change from one chord to another. A good example is your first finger when you change from A to D. Try playing this chord exercise without lifting your first finger from the third string, second fret.

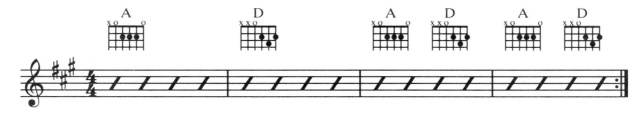

You can also think of your left-hand first finger as a pivot finger when you change chords from A to E7. As you move this finger down a fret, just release the pressure a bit and slide it down the string. This will have the effect of anchoring your hand as all your fingers move at once. Try playing through this pivot-finger exercise. To help you to concentrate on leading into each new chord with your first finger, play the first-finger note in between each chord as indicated by the ③, for third string, on the first beat of each measure. (If you are using your fingers to strum, use your thumb to play the single notes.)

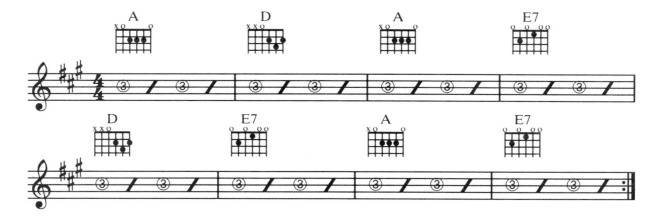

The Alternating Bass-Chord Strum

To make the bass-chord strum more lively and interesting, the following arrangement of "Old Joe Clark" makes use of a technique called *alternating bass*. Instead of always playing the primary bass note, you can alternate between primary bass and *secondary bass*. For the A chord, the secondary bass will be the open sixth string (⑥). While holding down the E7, use the fifth string (⑤) fretted at the second fret as a secondary bass.

This old-time hoedown song is based on a square-dance tune—so once you know it well, you should try to play it at a pretty good clip. Try practicing each measure individually by repeating it over and over to really get the smooth feel of this alternating-bass strum. This arrangement has both a *first* and *second ending:* When you get to the end, play the measure bracketed as **1.** Play the song again, then skip this measure and play the measure bracketed as **2** instead.

Old Joe Clark

Pivot Practice in A Major

Now play "Simple Gifts" using three chords—A, D, and E7. (These chords are the I, IV, and V7 chords in the key of A major.) This gentle Shaker hymn is a inspirational favorite which was repopularized by Judy Collins during the seventies. "Simple Gifts" lends itself well to a plain four-strums-per-bar accompaniment style. There's no need to lift your index finger from the third string as you change from chord to chord. Just slide this pivot finger along the string when you need to change frets.

Simple Gifts

The Flick

Here is an adaptation of the bass-chord strum that can add a lot of interest to an accompaniment. It is called "the flick" because you strum by flicking your index or middle finger down and up across the strings. On the downstroke, you should try to cover all of the strings except the primary bass. On the upstroke, you should strum lightly across only two or three strings. This is a great technique to learn because it sounds a lot like you are playing with a pick. After you master the flick with your fingers, you may want to go back and try it with a pick. This exercise will introduce you to the four different flick patterns you will need to know for the next tune. (Remember: ⊓ = downstroke and ∨ = upstroke.) Practice it slowly and evenly until you really get the feel of this swingy eighth-note accompaniment style.

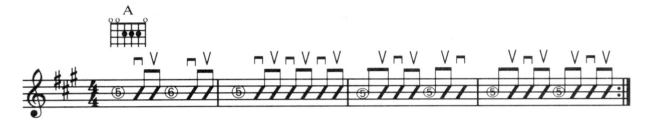

Now you are ready to try out the flick on "Old Joe Clark." Since you are familiar with the chord changes, you can give your full attention to making the right-hand part smooth. Notice that there are no alternating bass notes in the second half.

Old Joe Clark

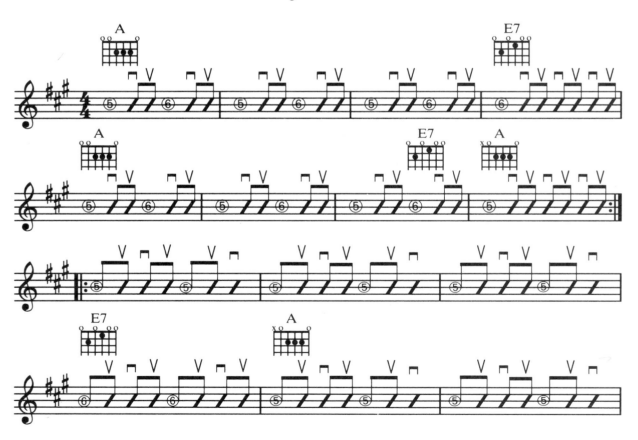

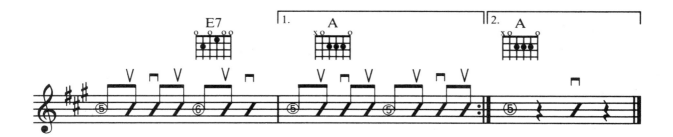

Waltz Time Strums

Let's explore strums that work well in $\frac{3}{4}$ time (waltz time). Here are a few eighth-note strumming patterns that you will need to play the next song.

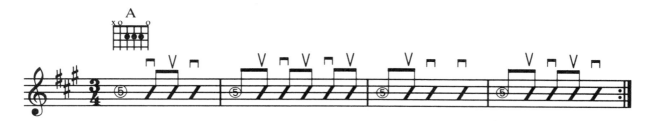

Now play the classic love song "Drink to Me Only With Thine Eyes" using the indicated strumming patterns. The symbol in the last measure is a *whole rest*. This symbol is also called a *measure rest*, because it indicates silence for an entire measure.

Drink to Me Only With Thine Eyes

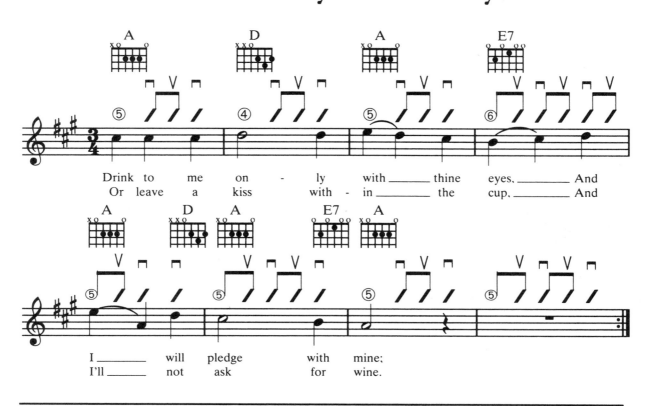

The Key of D Major

Even though it is possible to play thousands of songs with the three chords that you now know, you will want to learn other chords so that you can play songs in different keys. It is safe to say that you will continue to learn new chords throughout your study and performance career. Sometimes you may want to play a certain song in a certain key because it places that song in a good range for singing. With other songs, particular keys might make the guitar part easier to play.

The three most important chords in any key are the *I chord, IV chord,* and *V7 chord.* As their names imply, these chords are built on the first, fourth, and fifth degrees of the scale. You have already learned that in the key of A the I chord, IV chord, and V7 chord are A, D, and E7, respectively. In the key of D major, the I, IV, and V7 chords are D, G, and A7. First, let's look at the A7 chord, which is a simple variation of the A chord that you already know. The A7 chord serves as the V7 chord in the key of D major.

The A7 Chord

To turn an A chord into an A7, just lift your first finger off the third string. Strum the A7 chord a few times.

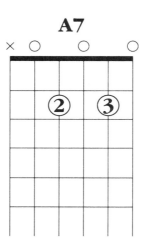

The G Chord

The G chord serves as the IV chord in the key of D major. Learning to play the G chord without any muted or buzzing strings may take a little practice. Be sure to keep your left wrist low so that you will be able to arch your left-hand fingers enough to fret each string with the fingertip. If you do have trouble getting the G chord to sound right, hold down the chord and play each string individually. When you find one string that sounds buzzy or muffled, adjust your hand position slightly until the problem goes away. Pretty soon you should be able to strum this full-sounding chord with confidence.

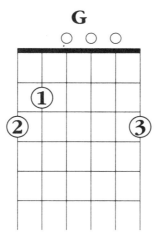

Pivot Practice in D Major

The D chord is the I chord in the key of D major. When you change from D to A7, just slide your third finger down one fret along the second string. When you change from D to G, just move your third finger from the second to the first string at the same fret. Remember to try to get all of your fingers to move at once—and to use your third finger as the reference point for the shape. Play this progression a few times to practice changing chords smoothly in the key of D.

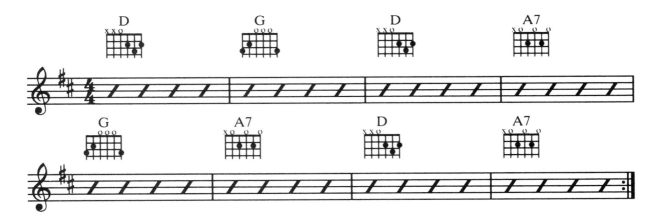

Syncopation

Syncopation is an important rhythmic technique in all kinds of music, especially jazz and rock. Simply speaking, a syncopated strum is an eighth-note strum in which you leave out some of the downstrokes. This has the effect of accenting the upstrokes, which fall on the *offbeats*. Two syncopated strum patterns are used in the following arrangement of "Sloop John B.," a West Indian folk song which became a favorite of the Beach Boys in 1966. Their recording of this classic tune stayed on the chart for ten weeks, topping at the third position. The syncopated strums help bring out the Calypso flavor of this lilting, syncopated melody. Try strumming the two patterns used in "Sloop John B." using the indicated chords. Notice that the second pattern is a bass-chord strum, with only one bass note per measure. You may find that playing one of the upstrokes as a downstroke (as indicated by the markings in parentheses) will help you to play this rhythm more steadily.

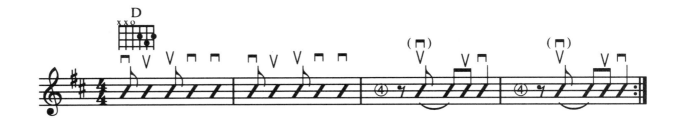

Now play "Sloop John B." at a moderate tempo. Use the first syncopated strum for the verse and the second pattern for the chorus. A *half rest* appears in the second half of measure 9. This rest is worth two beats.

Sloop John B.

Chorus

So hoist up the *John B.* sails,

See how the main-sail sets, Call for the cap-tain a - shore, let __ me go

home. Let __ me go home,

I want to go home. I feel so break ____ up

I want __ to go home.

The E7 Chord as II7

As you have learned, in the key of A, the E7 chord functions as the V7 chord (because it is built on the fifth note of the A major scale). Now that we are playing in the key of D, the E7 becomes a II7 chord (because it is built upon the second note of the D major scale). Practice this progression until you can change smoothly to each of these four chords in the key of D.

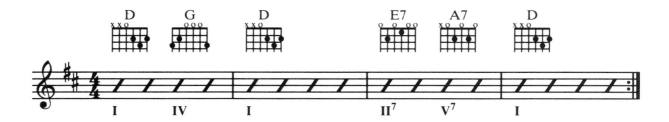

The II7 chord adds harmonic interest to this rock and roll version of "My Bonnie." Once you have mastered the syncopated strums as shown, try making up a few of your own.

My Bonnie

Playing Lead Guitar

The great lead-guitar players all know how to play a melody solo. This is the kind of lead playing that you got a chance to try earlier. It is also important to know how to *improvise* a solo—and that is what we are going to examine here.

The Blues Scale

An easy way to begin improvising your own lead breaks is to use the *pentatonic blues scale.* This five-note scale works well with most blues and rock chord progressions. It is so versatile that you will hear it in the playing of every notable guitarist, from Doc Watson to Randy Rhoads, from Blind Lemon Jefferson to Joe Satriani. Try playing the pentatonic blues scale in the key of A.

In "Good Morning Blues" you will get a chance to really get to know the pentatonic blues scale in A. The first time through you play the song's melody, and the second time you play a solo. If you are using a pick, you will notice that the picking indications guide you to play notes that are on the beat with downstrokes and notes that are on offbeats with upstrokes. This simple rule is a very good one to follow since it helps you to feel the natural accents of the music. If you are using your fingers to play this blues, make sure that you alternate your index and middle fingers. Once you feel familiar with the song, try making up your own solos over this progression. Stay within the pentatonic blues scale, but let your creativity guide you.

Good Morning Blues

Well, good morn - ing, blues, ___ blues, how do you do? ___

Well, good morn - ing, blues, ___ blues, how do you do?

Well, I'm do - ing all right, say, good

morn - ing, how ___ are you?

You will get some more practice with pentatonic scales in the "Developing Your Repertoire" section. But you can practice playing lead on your own, or with a friend: Any melody you come up with that uses the notes of the A pentatonic blues scale will work against most blues/rock chord progressions in the key of A.

Minor Chords

The chords that you have learned so far are all major chords. In this section, you'll get to play some *minor* chords, which have a somewhat sad or introspective sound. Because of these qualities, minor chords work well in love ballads—or any songs that create a personal portrait or call up visions of the past. After you have learned the two minor chords below, you will be able to play songs in the key of A minor.

The A Minor Chord

The A minor chord (abbreviated *Am*) has a very natural feel on the fretboard. Although the fingering is fairly different from that of the A major chord, there is only one different note: the one on the second string. In fact, all minor chords are only one note different from their major counterparts. Strum the Am chord a few times.

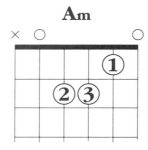

After you feel comfortable with the A minor chord, try strumming A major and A minor, as indicated in this chord exercise. Notice that your second finger acts as a pivot finger in this change.

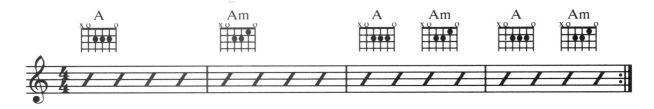

The D Minor Chord

The D minor chord (abbreviated *Dm*) has one different note from the D major chord: the note on the first string. Strum the Dm chord a few times.

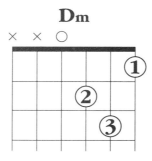

Try changing back and forth from D major to D minor using your third finger as a pivot finger.

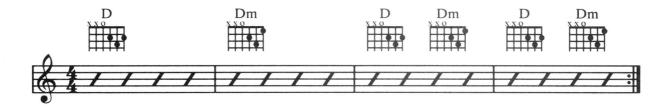

Chord Practice in A Minor

You will get a chance to practice the A minor and D minor chords, along with the G major chord, in "Johnny Has Gone for a Soldier." This affecting ballad (sometimes known as "Buttermilk Hill") has remained an American favorite since colonial times. It served as a popular Civil War song—and as a powerful song of protest during the Vietnam War. Play two half-note strums per measure as you practice changing to and from chords. Once you can play the song smoothly, you may want to experiment with other strums. In the third measure of the melody, you'll see a *dotted quarter note.* Placing a dot after a note increases that note's time value by one-half. So, a dotted quarter note is held for one-and-a-half beats.

Johnny Has Gone for a Soldier

Suspended Chords

When you change a basic three-note chord by adding an extra note or by substituting a different note for one of the regular chord tones, you are using a *chord embellishment*. There are many varieties of chord embellishments, the most common of which being seventh chords like the two that you have already learned (E7 and A7). The most common type of *substitution* is called a *suspended fourth chord* (abbreviated *sus4*).

The Dsus4 Chord

To play a Dsus4 chord, all you need to do is play a D chord and then move the note on the first string up one fret by putting down your fourth finger.

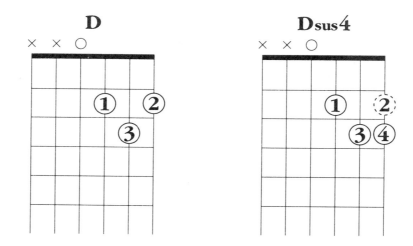

When you change chords from D major to Dsus4, you should leave your second finger down—even though it is no longer necessary to fret the string. This makes it easy to change back to D, because all you have to do is lift the fourth finger. As a general rule, if there is no need to lift a finger when changing from one chord to the next, don't do it. You will notice that the second finger on the first string, second fret is still indicated in the Dsus4 chord diagram to remind you of this rule.

Now try this D-to-Dsus4 strumming exercise.

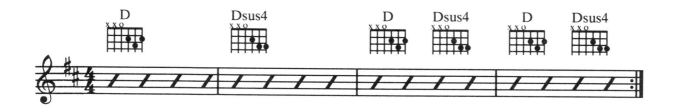

The Gsus4 Chord

Playing the Gsus4 chord requires a left-hand technique called *damping*. To damp a string is to muffle it with a finger of your left hand. In the Gsus4 chord, the fifth string shouldn't be played. The trick is to damp it by letting your third finger—which is fretting the sixth string, third fret—rest against it. When you strum across all the strings, you should not hear any sound from the fifth string. Play each string individually from low to high to make sure that you are damping the fifth string but that all the other notes sound clearly.

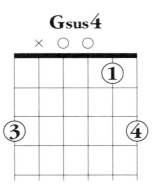

Since the Gsus4 chord usually precedes or follows the normal G chord, it makes sense to use a new fingering for the G that makes this change easy. This new fingering of the G chord produces the same notes as the one you already know. Many chord forms may have *alternate fingerings* such as this—the fingering you use depends on the context in which a particular chord is played.

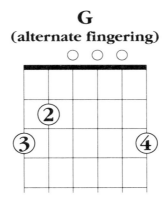

After you have practiced these two new chords a bit, try changing back and forth from G to Gsus4. Since your third and fourth fingers fret the same notes in both chords, just keep them planted firmly when changing from one chord to the other.

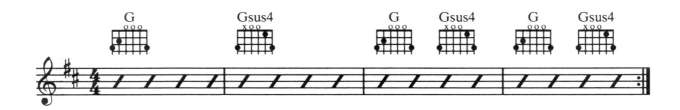

The A7sus4 Chord

The A7sus4 chord is formed by adding your fourth finger to the A7 chord.

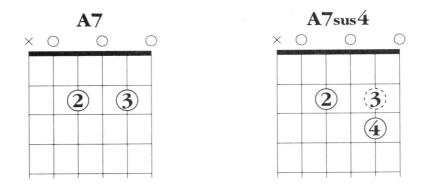

You should leave your third finger down as you change from A7 to A7sus4 in this exercise.

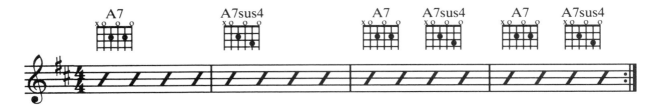

Suspended Chord Practice

The following arrangement of "Silent Night" uses the three suspended chords you have just learned. This beloved Christmas carol was first heard on Christmas Day, 1818, in St. Nicholas Church in the village of Oberdorf, Austria. The curate, Joseph Mohr, had penned the words the night before and asked the organist, Franz Gruber, to write the music. Since the organ at the church had broken down, this first performance was accompanied on guitar.

The melody of "Silent Night" features *dotted half notes,* as well as dotted quarter notes. The dotted half note is held for three beats—and the dotted quarter note is held for one-and-a-half beats. Play "Silent Night" with the indicated strumming pattern, and watch for the changes to the sus4 chords. When you can play it smoothly, try varying the strumming pattern and the points at which the sus4s are added.

Silent Night

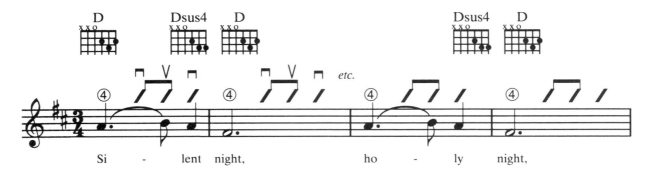

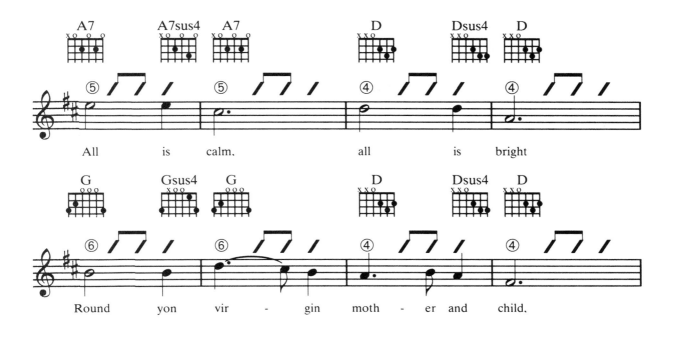

All is calm, all is bright

Round yon vir - gin moth - er and child,

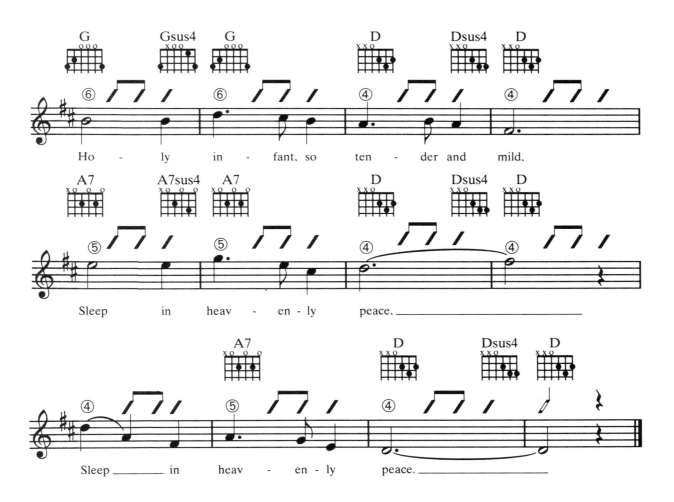

Ho - ly in - fant, so ten - der and mild,

Sleep in heav - en - ly peace,_____

Sleep _____ in heav - en - ly peace. _____

Playing Broken-Chord Accompaniment

Broken-chord accompaniment, also called *arpeggio style,* is a way to play chords one or two notes at a time. This style is usually used on slow to moderate-tempo songs to provide a gentle, flowing accompaniment. There are several different right-hand techniques for producing this effect—depending on whether you want to use a pick, your fingers, or a combination of both.

Picks and Fingers

It is easy to play basic broken-chord accompaniments with your fingers: You simply play a bass note with your thumb, and then follow it with single notes played by the index, middle, and (sometimes) ring fingers. If you use a pick, you have two options: You can play all of the notes in the broken-chord pattern with the pick (using alternating upstrokes and downstrokes), or you can play the first bass note with the pick, and the remaining notes in the pattern with your middle and ring fingers.

In the exercises and songs that follow, you will find right-hand fingering guides for each of the three methods outlined above. You should at least try each one of the methods once or twice to determine which one feels and sounds the most natural to you. When you play a broken chord with your fingers, you should use *free strokes* instead of rest strokes. To execute a free stroke, allow the tip of your finger to curl slightly after it has sounded the string so that it ends up in the air rather than resting on the next lower string. This technique lets all the notes of the chord ring out. Start out slowly and make sure that you give equal time value to each note in the four patterns.

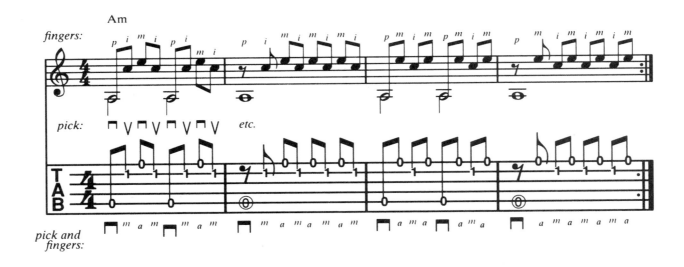

"Johnny Has Gone for a Soldier" sounds great with broken-chord accompaniment. Since you are already familiar with the chord progression, you can pay full attention to getting your right hand moving smoothly. Add a little bit of emphasis to the bass notes to create a nice feeling of phrasing in this gentle ballad.

Johnny Has Gone for a Soldier

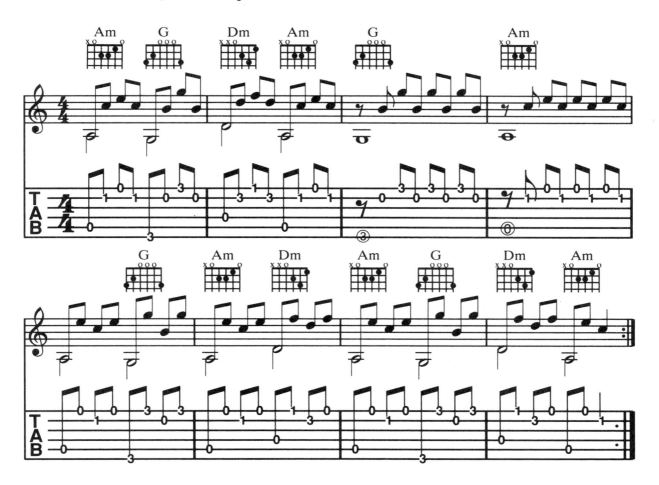

Broken Chords in Waltz Time

Now try some arpeggio patterns in $\frac{3}{4}$ time (waltz time). This exercise features alternating primary and secondary bass notes.

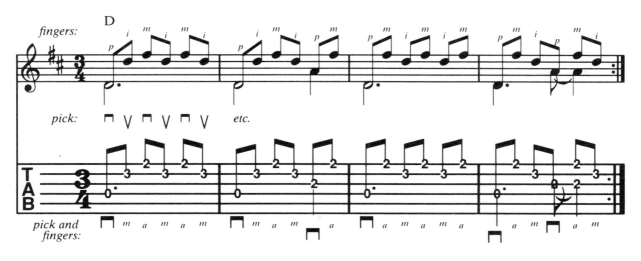

Now play "Silent Night" using broken-chord accompaniment. Notice how the arpeggio pattern in each measure has been chosen to accentuate the change to the sus4 chord on the third beat. Once you can play this song smoothly, try varying the patterns. The squiggly line in front of the last chord means you should play a slow downstroke strum with your thumb.

Silent Night

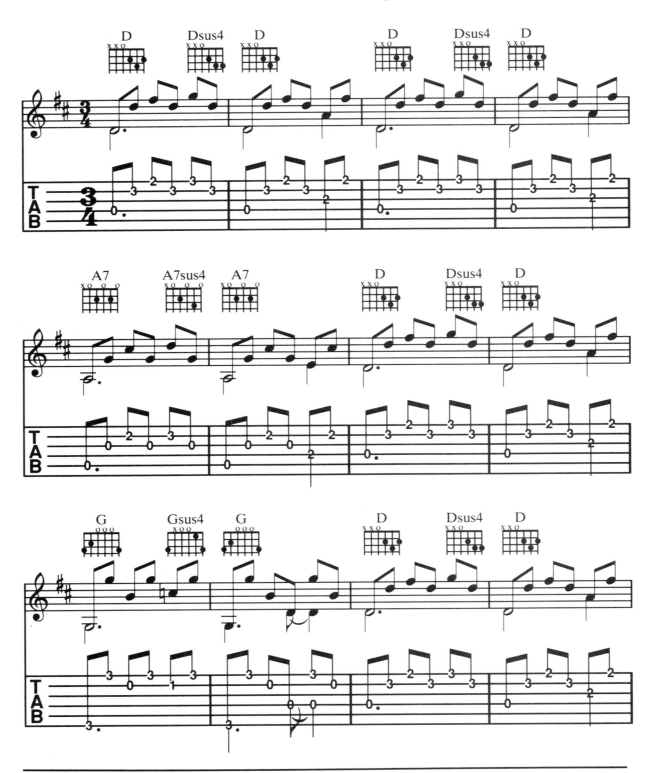

The Key of G Major

So far, you have played songs in the keys of A, D, and A minor. By learning just three new chords, you can play many new songs in the key of G major. You already know the G chord and D chord, which function as the I and V chords in the key of G. In this section, you'll learn the G7, D7, and C chords, which function as the I7, V7, and IV chords in this important major key.

The G7 Chord

The G7 chord functions as I7 in the key of G. Strum the G7 chord a few times.

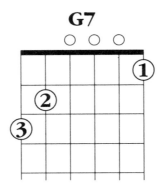

The C Chord

The C chord may seem a bit difficult at first because of the placement of the first finger. As always, practice bringing all of the fingers down at once to really get the feeling of the chord shape. The C chord acts as the IV chord in the key of G major.

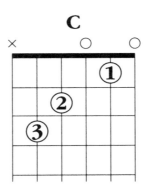

The D7 Chord

The D7 chord acts as the V7 in the key of G. Be sure not to sound either string marked with an **X** when you strum this chord.

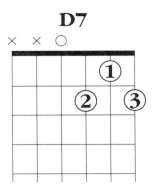

D7

Chord Practice in G Major

Get ready to practice the new chords you have just learned in the key of G major. To make the change from G to G7, begin with the alternate fingering of the G chord which you learned for "Silent Night" (using fingers 2-3-4). Leave your second and third fingers in place when you make the change to G7. To make the change smoothly, you can get your first finger in place for the G7 before lifting your fourth finger. When you change from G7 to C or from C to G7, work on moving your second and third fingers together as a unit. In making the change from D7 to C, you should leave your first finger down as a pivot finger. In the more difficult change from G to D7 and back to G, you can think of your index finger as a *lead finger*; since it is not used in the G chord, you can get it almost in place for the D7 and let it lead you into the new chord. In changing back to G, leave your first finger down as long as possible to give you a reference point for forming the new chord.

Now you're ready to play "Amazing Grace" in the key of G Major. This beloved hymn was written in the late 1700s by John Newton, a reformed slave-trader who saw the light and became a minister. As a tribute to the lasting popularity of this song, Judy Collins made it a top-40 hit in 1971. The following year, the Royal Scots Dragoon Guards of Scotland's armored regiment recorded a bagpipe band version of the tune that put it back on the pop charts. Bill Moyers recently chose this meaningful song as the subject of a documentary special, featuring Jean Ritchie, Judy Collins, and Johnny Cash.

Draw out some of the downstrokes of your flick strums to give a bit of an arpeggio effect to this beautiful hymn.

Amazing Grace

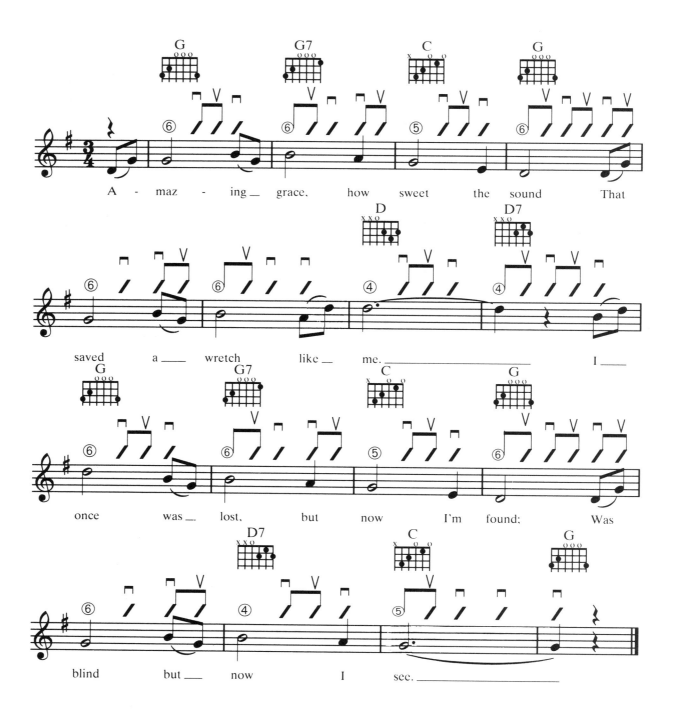

The Key of C Major

By learning one more chord, you can play many songs in the key of C major. You already know the C chord and the G7 chord, which serve as the I and V7 chords in the key of C. Take a look now at the F chord, which functions as the IV chord in this important major key.

The F Chord

The F chord shown below is what is known as a *bar chord*. To play the full chord you use your index finger to bar across all the strings so that it frets the first, second, and sixth strings at the first fret. Position your index finger so that the tip is just covering the sixth string as you lay it flat across all the strings. You may find it easier to get the first-finger notes to sound clearly if you roll your first finger back slightly. Check that your thumb is in the middle of the back of the neck and opposite the second fret. This will allow you to exert the most pressure with the first finger.

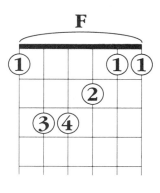

If you have trouble getting a good sound out of the F chord, use this alternate fingering at first. It is much easier to play because the index finger bars only two strings.

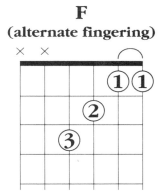

Practice changing from the C chord to the F chord. As you make this change, don't let your thumb move. Use your third finger as a pivot. (If you are using the alternate fingering for F, you can pivot on your index finger.) Once you are familiar with this change, play "Oh, Susanna" in the key of C. This song will give you a chance to practice playing the I, II7, IV, and V7 chords in the key of C: that's the C, D7, F, and G7 chords. James Taylor made this well-known American song even more famous on his well-known pop album, *Sweet Baby James*. Once you have mastered this arrangement in the key of C, you may want to experiment with different strumming patterns. Or try varying the spots at which the alternate fingering for the F chord is used.

Oh, Susanna

Playing Fingerstyle

So far, there have always been instructions for your using either your fingers or a pick. In this section you will get a chance to work on using your fingers alone. There is a long and distinguished tradition of fingerstyle playing (also called *fingerpicking*) that stretches from the earliest Renaissance and baroque works—to the great country blues players—right up to today's jazz and new age masters. You did some fingerstyle playing when you played the arpeggio accompaniments to "Johnny Has Gone for a Soldier" and "Silent Night." The difference in the following pieces is that they may be played as solos, because you will be playing both melody and accompaniment. This is accomplished by getting your right-hand fingers to work independently of your thumb.

"Dead Thumb" Picking

The easiest fingerstyle technique is called *"dead thumb"* style because you play a steady bassline using only the primary bass note of each chord. In the following exercise, your left-hand third and fourth fingers play a simple melody above the E7 and A7 chords, as diagrammed.

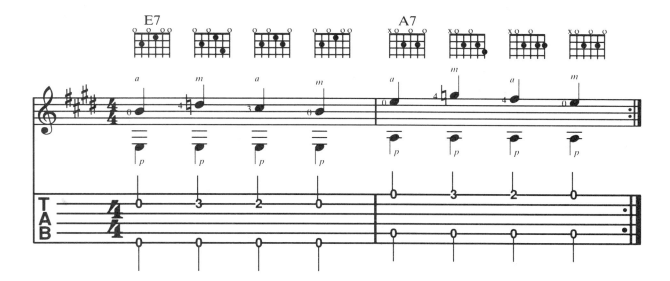

Hammerons

A *hammeron* is a left-hand technique you can use to add polish and variety to an accompaniment part or a solo. This technique involves producing a tone without picking the string with the right hand. The dead-thumb exercise below features hammerons on an E7 chord. You'll use a similar pattern later when you play the Texas-blues song "Sugar Babe." The curved line that connects the first two treble notes is a *slur*, and tells you to play the second note as a hammeron. First, finger the E7 chord normally. Then, lift up your first finger so that you can play the third string open. After playing the open third string with your right-hand index finger (together with the open sixth string played by the thumb), bring your left-hand first finger down on the string to sound the first-fret note. (This is a lot easier to do than it is to describe.) Try it a few times to get the feel. (Pay careful attention to your timing to make sure that the "hammered on" note falls exactly in between two bass notes.)

You can also hammer on from one fretted note to another. To see how this works, try the same pattern using the A7 chord. Finger the A7 chord as you normally would, but put your left-hand first finger down on the second string at the first fret. Play this note first (together with the open fifth string played by the thumb), and then hammer on to the second string, second fret with your third finger.

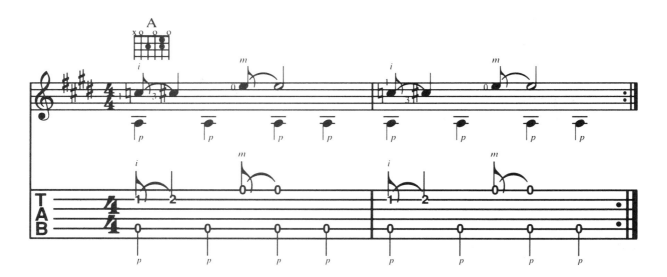

The B7 Chord

To play "Sugar Babe," you'll need the B7 chord, which is the V7 chord in the key of E. Place all four fingers as shown in the diagram and strum across all five strings.

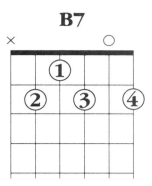

B7

Slides

A *slide* is another left-hand technique that you can use to dress up a song. Take a look at the slide found in the last two measures of "Sugar Babe." These measures form a *turnaround* lick that you can play at the end of most any blues song. The straight line before the first note of the turnaround tells you to slide up to that note from one or two frets below. Fret the third string with your second finger at the second fret. Play the note and quickly slide your second finger along the string up to the fourth to sound the written note. Then play the rest of the turnaround as written.

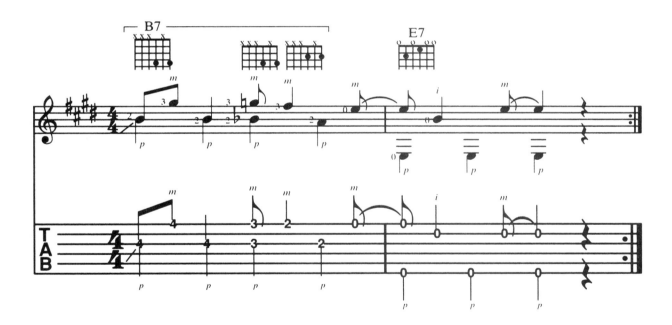

Now play the complete arrangement of "Sugar Babe," which is called an *eight-bar blues* because a complete verse of the song is eight measures long. This great, old country-blues song is associated with Texas blues master Mance Lipscomb.

Sugar Babe

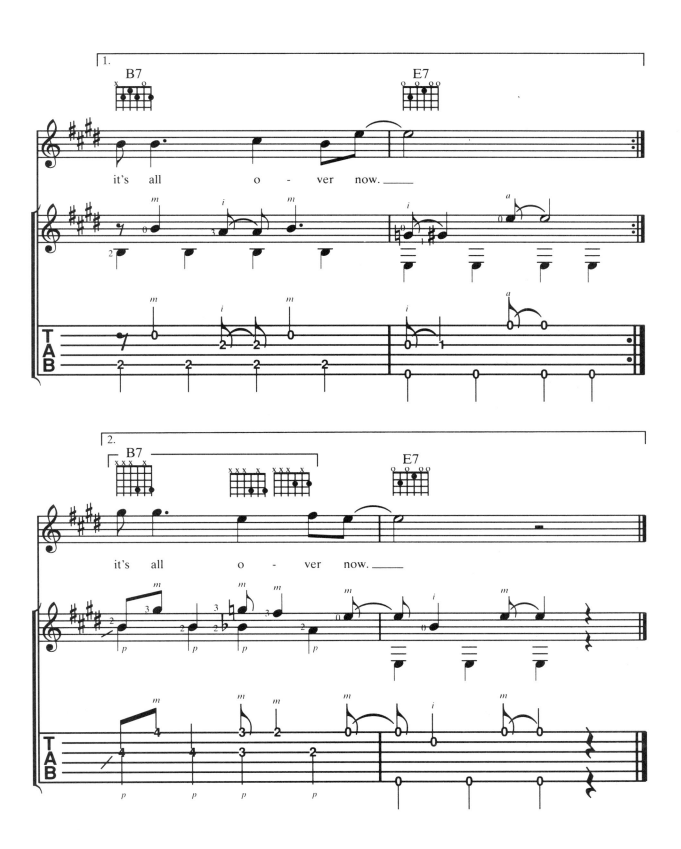

Pattern Picking

As you know, in the alternating bass style, your right-hand thumb must alternate between the primary bass and a secondary bass for each chord. The following arrangement of "Railroad Bill" features a type of alternating bass picking called *pattern picking*. While your thumb keeps the steady alternating bass going, your fingers repeat the same pattern of treble notes for each measure.

There are many versions of "Railroad Bill" in the annals of American folk song—but they all tell the story of a rough character who "never worked, and he never will." This is a version that is associated with superpickers like Doc and Merle Watson. Although there are a couple of new chord forms in this arrangement, each is quite similar to one your already know. Practice these new forms.

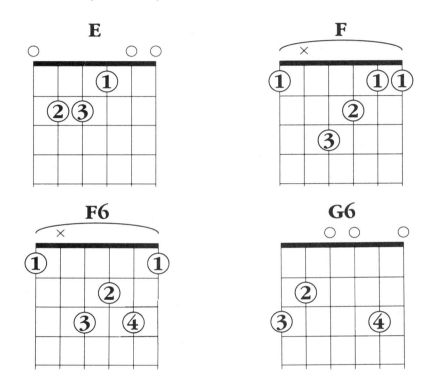

The entire arrangement sticks to an unvarying right-hand pattern, but by adding a few embellishments to the standard chords in the key of C, you can outline the basic melody of the song. Notice that in the first three measures you need to add your fourth finger (on the first string, third fret) to the C chord. Throughout most of this arrangement, the treble notes are on the first and second strings. In the sixth measure, the pattern shifts to the second and third strings and stays on these strings for two more measures. This happens again in the last two measures. Play "Railroad Bill" at a slow, steady tempo until you can play the pattern evenly and automatically—then step up the tempo gradually.

Railroad Bill

Rail - road __ Bill,

Bill, He nev - er worked, and __

he nev - er will. Gon - na ride on, ___

Rail - road _____ Bill. _____

Developing Your Repertoire

Now that you've got the basics of guitar playing under your belt, you're ready to start adding songs to your *repertoire*—which is simply the list of songs that you can play with confidence. In fact, learning new songs is the most enjoyable way for a developing guitarist to strengthen playing skills and explore new territory.

In the sections that follow, you'll find guitar arrangements for hit songs in several musical styles—blues, rock, pop, jazz, and classical. As you play the songs that follow, you'll use skills you learned in previous sections. You will also learn new guitar techniques that will add style to your playing. Even if you have a special interest in only one or two of these types of music—you'll benefit from playing the songs in each section.

The Blues

The blues was born in the American South. It evolved from the work songs written by Black-American slaves before the Civil War—and so bears the influence of African rhythms and tonality. The blues is known for its power to evoke the listener's emotions—because its lyric often tells a personal story of troubles and longing. The plaintive melody and harmony of the blues, coupled with its strong and simple rhythm, make it a universally appealing musical form.

Frankie and Johnny

"Frankie and Johnny" is perhaps the most famous blues of all time. This stark tale of love and murder was recorded by many great blues artists—and was a signature tune for Mae West. As a testament to this song's versatility, R&B singer/songwriter Brook Benton put it on the charts for four weeks in 1961; soul singer Sam Cooke put it on the charts for seven weeks in 1963; and Elvis Presley, the King of Rock and Roll, made it a hit once again for five weeks in 1966.

The rhythm of "Frankie and Johnny" is what is known as a *shuffle rhythm*. This means that the first eighth note in each group of two is held for a slightly longer time than the second. This gives a bouncy blues feel to both melody and accompaniment. The way to get this feeling into your strumming is to think of each quarter-note beat as being divided into three. When there are three notes per beat, they are written as an *eighth-note triplet,* with a *3* over the beam. Try this simple exercise that starts out in quarter notes and goes to eighth-note triplets. Count out loud and keep a steady beat as you play.

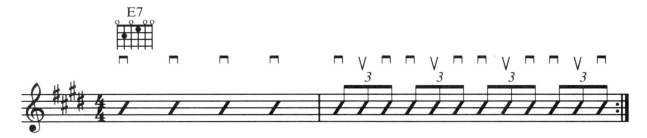

To produce the typical shuffle rhythm, you play only the first and third note in each eighth-note triplet. Try this rhythm with the E7 chord.

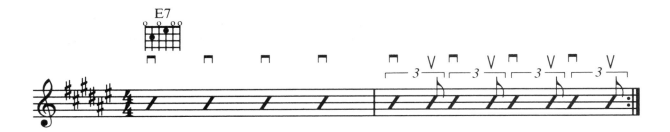

Now try playing the chords and chord embellishments used in "Frankie and Johnny." Just add your third finger to the E7 to form E13, and your fourth finger to A7 to form A13. The bluesy, dissonant C7 is just the B7 form slid up one fret.

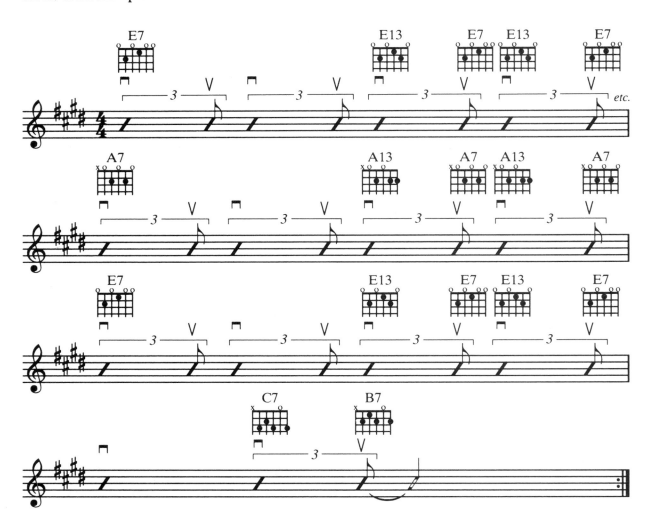

Since the shuffle rhythm is continued throughout the entire song, it is cleaner to write the part out in eighth notes and place the following marking at the top of the piece.

In the second ending of "Frankie and Johnny," you will find another classic blues turnaround riff. Practice this riff with your left-hand first and second fingers in the positions shown, and then play the whole song.

Frankie and Johnny

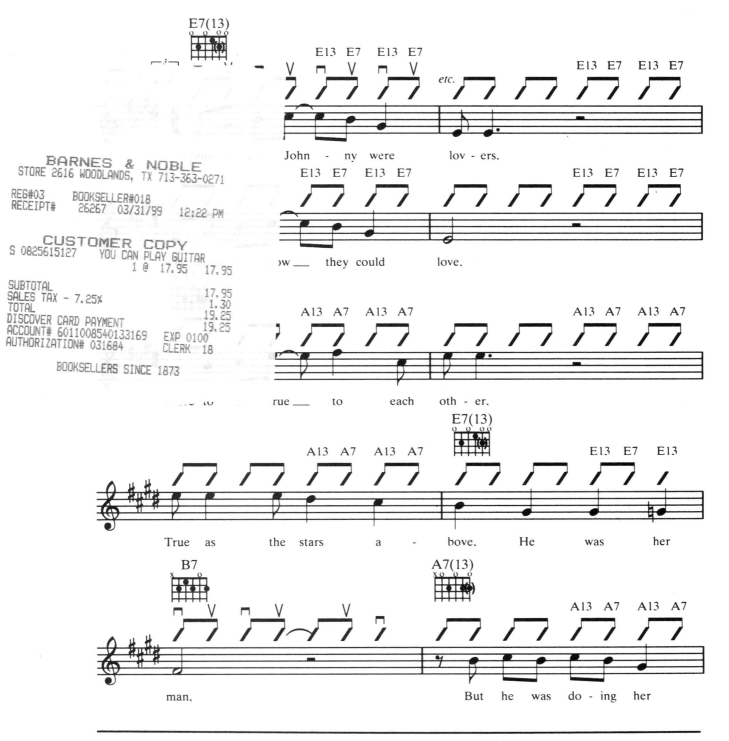

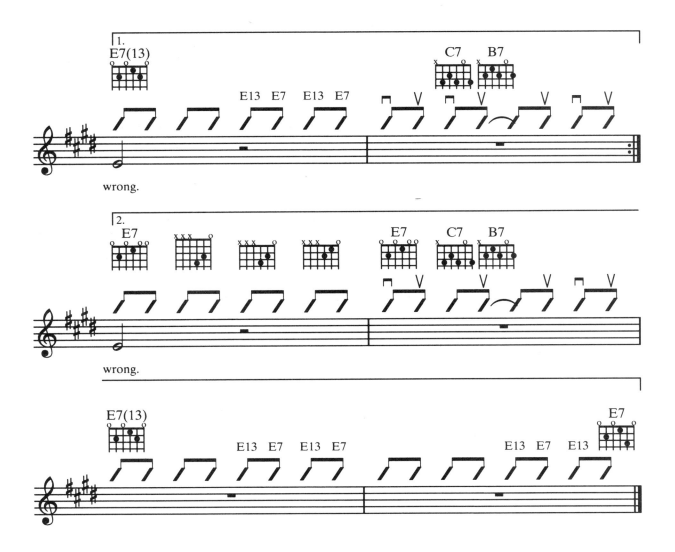

wrong.

wrong.

C.C. Rider

"C.C. Rider" is an all-time favorite blues and rock hit that has been performed by a wide range of artists. Ma Rainey brought this tune to position fourteen on the charts in 1925. In 1957, rhythm and blues singer Chuck Willis had a career-making hit with this song—and inspired the dance craze called "The Stroll." In 1963, rhythm and blues singer LaVern Baker recorded her hit version of this tune ("See See Rider"). The magic had still not worn off this terrific rhythm number—for Eric Burdon & the Animals made "See See Rider" a hit once again for seven weeks in 1966.

In the backup part to "C.C. Rider," you get to play what is known as a *Memphis shuffle,* which uses straight eighth notes. To play this versatile backup riff, you will need to stretch a bit: The basic chord position of the Memphis shuffle involves a three-fret stretch between your left-hand first and second fingers. Then you have to put your left-hand fourth finger down two frets and even three frets above your second finger. Before you play the song, try this stretching exercise. Use all downstrokes and make sure that you are damping all of the open strings. Keep your second finger down while you are playing the fourth-finger notes. Once you are familiar with this exercise, try playing it on the fourth and fifth strings as well.

Now, follow the fingering carefully as you play this blues classic. Notice that many of the chord positions will not fit in standard diagrams because they go above the fifth fret. In these diagrams, a Roman numeral gives you the first-finger fret number as a reference.

C.C. Rider

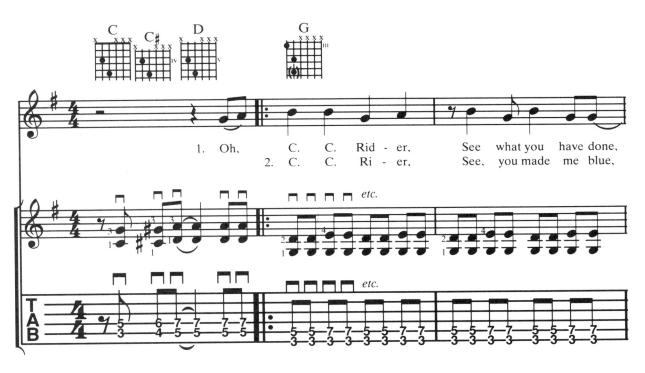

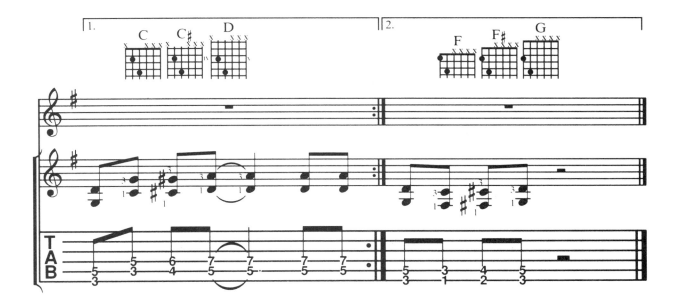

Rock

Rock and roll emerged in the 1950s as "rockabilly" music—a blending of hillbilly-style country music and the driving beat of Black rhythm & blues. Rock's pioneers include Bill Haley, Carl Perkins, Chuck Berry, Elvis Presley, Jerry Lee Lewis, and Little Richard. By the late 1950s, rock and roll was no longer a novelty, but had entered the pop mainstream—with millions of avid fans in American and Europe. In the 1960s, the popularity of rock music was brought to a new peak with the advent of British rock groups, beginning with the Beatles. Other British groups, like the Who and the Rolling Stones, followed soon after. Lots of different rock forms have evolved over the years, including acid rock, glitter rock, southern rock, and heavy metal—but the one thing that all of these forms have in common is that they all depend on the sound of the guitar.

In this section, you'll get to play two classic rock uptunes—hits for Cream and Los Lobos. As you perform each of these tunes, you'll see the close relationship between rock and its parent forms—blues and rhythm & blues.

La Bamba

Latin rock and roll star Ritchie Valens had a hit with "La Bamba" in 1959. The movie based on his life, *La Bamba,* was released in 1987—with music by the Latin-American rock quintet Los Lobos. Their version of this terrific Latin tune held the number one position on the charts for three weeks. The simple I-IV-V chord progression of "La Bamba" has been used for countless rock songs over the years; in fact, you can use the following arrangement to play songs such as "Twist and Shout," "Good Lovin'," and "Do You Love Me."

In this arrangement of "La Bamba," you will learn an essential method of rock backup. The use of *power chords* is a simple way for a guitarist to provide a hard-driving rock sound to a song. A power chord differs from other chords in that it consists of only the root and fifth of the chord. This is why the chord symbol for a power chord is followed by a **5.** There are six different power chords used in "La Bamba," but you use the same fingering for all of them. Place the first finger on the lower string and the third finger two frets up on the higher string.

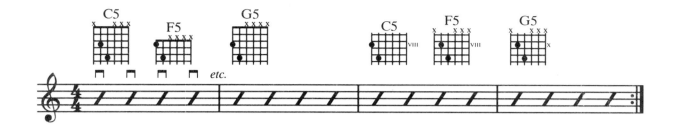

These positions are known as *moveable* chord forms because they do not use any open strings. This means that they may be moved to any position on the fretboard. The **X** mark in the strumming notation tells you to damp the strings as you strum. This adds even more syncopation to this exciting accompaniment style. The strumming pattern repeats every two measures—so once you've mastered the first two measures, you pretty much know the whole song.

La Bamba

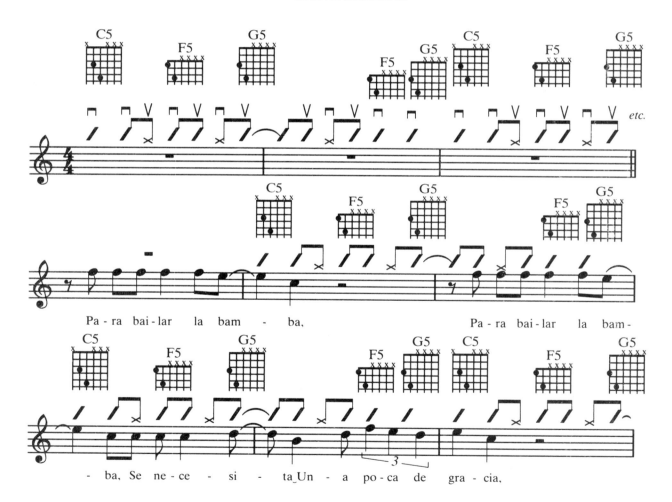

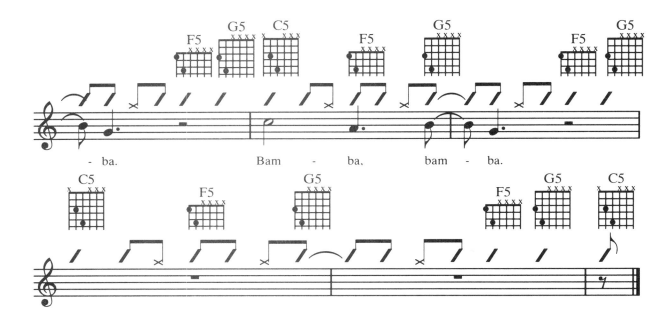

- ba.   Bam - ba,   bam - ba.

Crossroads

"Crossroads" is a traditional blues tune that Cream turned into a rock and roll hit in 1969. Originally entitled "Crossroad Blues," this song was a favorite of blues master Robert Johnson. Here's a blues-rock version of "Crossroads" that brings out its driving beat. In the introduction, you get to play a single-note riff that is similar to the one that Eric Clapton played in Cream's version. This riff is made up of notes taken from a first-position A blues scale.

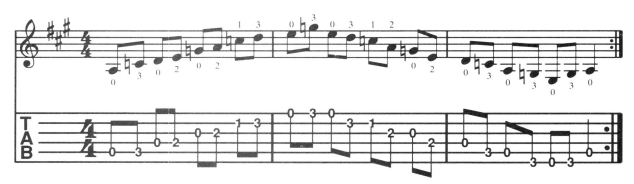

The one new technique in this riff is the *pulloff,* which is the opposite of a hammeron. Fret an A note on the third string, second fret using your second finger. Play the note, then pluck the string with your left-hand second finger so that you sound the open third string. The symbol for a pulloff is a slur—the same as for a hammeron: You know that this is a pulloff because it is going from one note to a lower note—a hammeron must go from one note to a higher note.

In the riff, this pulloff is followed by a hammeron back to the second fret.

The notation of this riff includes a new type of note called a *sixteenth note*. The time value of a sixteenth note is half that of an eighth note, or one-quarter of a quarter note. When you count a measure of eighth notes, you say, "One and, two and, three and, four and." When you count sixteenth notes, you need two extra syllables per beat, so you say, "One ee and ah, two ee and ah, three ee and ah, four ee and ah." Count and play this simple sixteenth-note example.

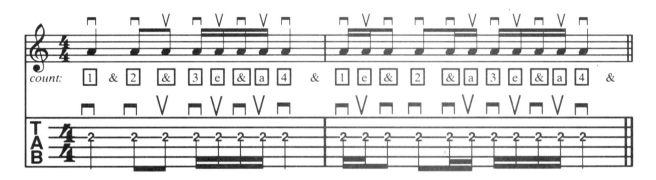

Now try playing the "Crossroads" signature riff. Count out loud as indicated until you can play it smoothly and solidly.

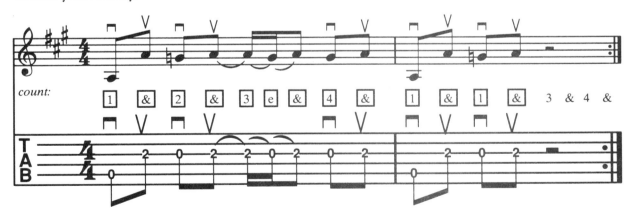

After the four-measure introduction, this arrangement has you playing a rhythm part for the first time through the verse. Here are the patterns that you play on the A and D chords. Notice the new fingerings for these chords as shown in the music. Use a four-string bar for the A and a three-string bar for D. You can play the riff with just the two bottom notes on each strum—or include some of the notes in parentheses on some or all of the strums.

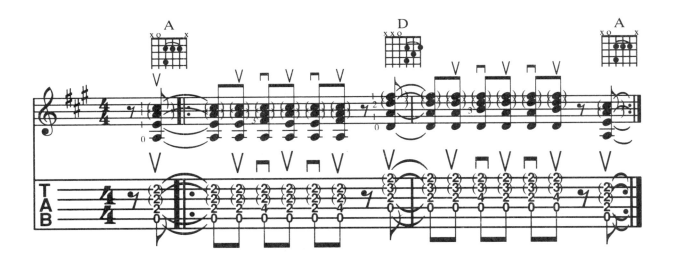

These rhythm parts alternate with the riff until measures 11 and 12, in which you use power chords on the D and E. (Notice that you can play the sixth string open on the E power chord to add extra fullness to the sound.)

The second time through the verse, it's a guitar solo. Before you try the solo as written, take a look at the blues scale on which it is based. This is called a *sliding scale* because it changes position every few notes. A scale like this gives you a lot more range than the single-position scales you have learned so far. Pay careful attention to the left-hand fingering as you play this scale up and down a few times.

You may have noticed that this scale has more than five notes per octave. Although it sounds a lot like a pentatonic blues scale, this scale is a bit more sophisticated because it includes an extra note. This note is called the *flatted fifth* (E♭ in the key of A), and it makes for a nice bit of bluesy chromaticism between the D and E notes.

The solo starts off with a slide on the third string into the E note on the ninth fret. Since you are coming off the A note on the second fret of the third string, start moving your second finger up the string toward the ninth fret and pick the string when your finger is somewhere around the sixth or seventh fret. The important thing is to arrive at the ninth-fret E note on time. In the following measure, there is a wavy line above the whole-note A (tenth fret, second string). This symbol indicates *vibrato*. As you hold the note, shake your hand back and forth in line with the guitar neck. This produces a slight variation in pitch and intensity of the held note. For a more pronounced type of vibrato, you can shake your finger up and down (perpendicular to the neck). Experiment with these two types of vibrato as you are learning this solo.

The solo also includes some *note bending*. All guitarists, except for classical players, use note bending to some extent—and it is a distinctively important technique in blues, rock, and country playing. When you bend a note, you raise its pitch by pushing up on the string with your fretting finger. This is easiest to do on electric guitars, which are usually strung with lighter gauge strings than other types of guitars. If you have an acoustic steel-string guitar, bending notes may hurt your fingers a bit, but you should be able to get good results. On a nylon-string guitar, it will be somewhat difficult to get the bends to sound right because the notes don't sustain as long as on a steel-string or electric and you cannot bend the pitch up quite as far. In this solo we will stick to bends that work well on any kind of guitar.

A bend is often followed by a *release;* that is, playing the bent note and then letting the pitch return to normal by releasing the upward finger pressure. This is just what happens in the second measure of the solo. The most important aspect of playing both bends and releases is to play them in tune. You have to know the pitch to which you are bending, and—once you get there—you have to hold the note at that pitch until you release it. Here is an exercise to help you develop your ear for bending. In the first half of the exercise, you play four fretted notes. In the second half, you play the same pitches by bending up to the second note and releasing down to the last note. Notice that the notation for bent notes shows you the pitch in parentheses in both the standard notation and tablature.

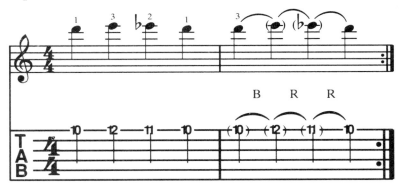

In the solo, the timing of this bend-and-release figure includes two *grace notes*—small notes that look like eighth notes with slashes through their flags. A grace note steals its time value from the preceding note's value. This means that you play the grace note a little before the note that follows it, so that you can arrive on that following note on the beat.

In the sixth measure of the solo there is the notation for a *prebend.* This indicates that you should play a bent note without first playing the natural fretted note. It takes a bit of practice to hit the bent note right in tune—but in this case you have a head start since it is similar to the bend and release that you played in the second measure. Notice that both the standard notation and tablature show you the pitch of the fretted note, even though it is not sounded until the bend is released.

The rest of the solo contains a pulloff figure and another bend-and-release figure. After you have learned both the backup and solo parts of this song, try making up your own variations of each part.

Crossroads

Introduction

I went down to the cross - roads, fell down on ___ my

knees,

I asked the Lord to have mer - cy,

save me if ___ you please.

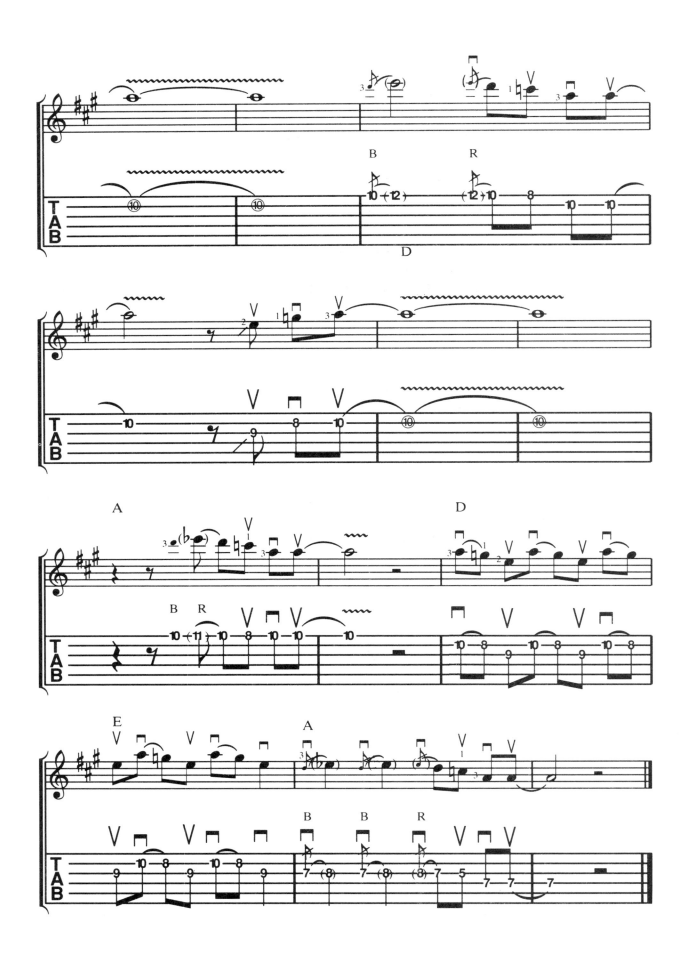

Pop

Generally speaking, any song or instrumental piece that enjoys wide commercial popularity is considered "pop" music—and the relative success of a pop song is measured by its rank on the pop charts. Contemporary pop and rock musics developed during the 1950s. Early pop music took several forms: there were "doo-wop" groups (like the Marcels and the Five Satins); close-harmony vocal ensembles (like the Supremes and Shirelles); and close-harmony groups doing "surf" music (notably, the Beach Boys and Jan and Dean).

Throughout the sixties and seventies, pop drew more and more influence from rock music—and today, many pop chart hits are actually rock, pop-rock, or "soft rock" music. The music of pop artists like Prince, Madonna, and Michael Jackson combines the harmonious and bright qualities of pop music with the driving beat, bold instrumentation, and special effects of rock music. Today's pop-rock hits are usually dance tunes—and feature strong and evocative rhythms. In this section, you'll focus on hits of the classic pop period as you play the music of Cat Stevens and Elvis Presley.

Morning Has Broken

"Morning Has Broken" is a traditional hymn that captured the attention of Cat Stevens. In 1972, his hit recording of this beautiful tune stayed on the pop charts for eleven weeks, peaking at position six. To bring out the gentle, yet insistent, rhythm of the song, you can use a broken-chord fingerpicking accompaniment. The pattern shown provides a steady flow of eighth notes. Notice that the secondary bass of each chord is the note found on the third string. This means that your right-hand thumb has to travel a bit on those chords whose root is on the fifth or sixth string.

In "Morning Has Broken," you will use four new chords. Three of these are *slash chords*. *F/C* means "F chord with a C note in the bass," *G/B* means "G chord with a B note in the bass," and *Em7/B* means "E minor seven chord with a B note in the bass." The selective use of different chord tones as primary basses can lend a lot of movement to a simple pattern like this one.

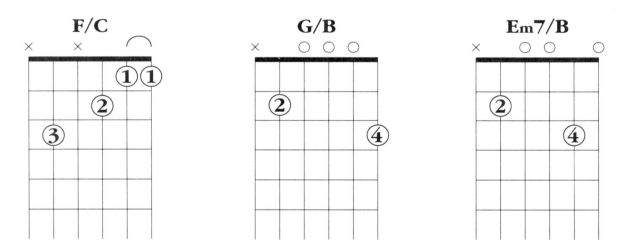

The fourth new chord is D7sus4—which you should be able to figure out for yourself by now. Practice the piece slowly and evenly, and remember that the left-hand fingering given in the music and the chord diagrams are there if you get into trouble.

Morning Has Broken

Morn-ing has brok en like the first

D.S. al Fine
(Go back to 𝄋 and play up
to "Fine".)

Aura Lee (Love Me Tender)

"Aura Lee" (composed by George R. Poulton) has long been considered one of America's most popular love melodies—and it enjoyed a smash revival in 1956 when Elvis Presley recorded it as "Love Me Tender." This chart-busting hit was the title song for Elvis's first movie—and stayed in the number one position on the charts for five weeks. This popular tune made it back on the charts when Richard Chamberlain recorded it in 1962—and again, as recorded by Percy Sledge in 1967.

The broken-chord pattern used for "Aura Lee" sounds very simple, but it has a new twist in that it requires you to play two treble notes together. If you are using a pick, there are two methods you can use to play the pattern: playing all of the notes with alternating pick strokes, with a two- or three-note strum on the two high strings; or playing both the third-string notes and the strums with your middle finger.

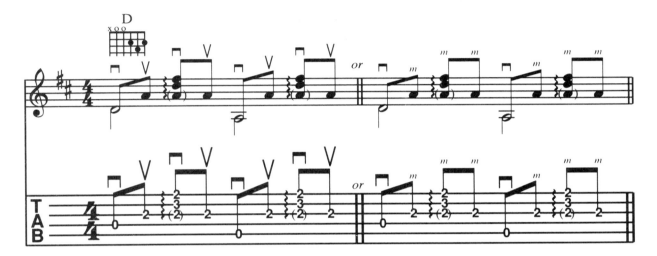

Even if you are going to play this pattern with your fingers, you may want strum the top strings with your middle finger if you are having trouble getting your middle and ring fingers to work together.

There are several new chords used in this song, and most of them are moveable chord forms because they contain no open strings. Notice that in the chord diagrams for moveable chords the string on which the root of the chord is played is marked by the letter **R.** If you know the names of the notes on the fifth and sixth strings, you can make new chords by sliding these forms up or down the neck to new positions. The "m7" designation in the chords Bm7, Gm7, and Em7 stands for "minor seven"—a minor chord with a seventh added. The "maj7" in the chord symbol Gmaj7 stands for "major seven"—this is a jazzy sounding embellishment to a major chord that is quite different from the standard seventh chords you have learned. The F♯7 (pronounced "F-sharp seven"), Bm7, and the new form for B7 are all bar chords, like the F chord that you already know. In the Gm7, you have to do a bar with your third finger. This feels awkward at first, but it makes it easy to damp the fifth and first strings. If you have trouble with this chord, you can use the alternate fingering shown. Here are all of the new chords used in "Aura Lee" for you to practice.

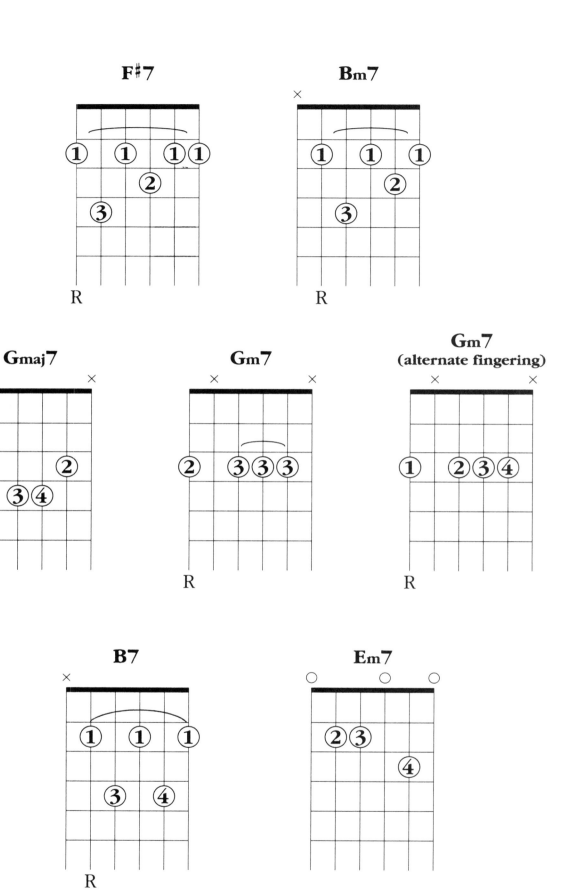

Once you are familiar with these chords, play "Aura Lee."

Aura Lee

Ragtime and Jazz

Most historians agree that jazz is a direct descendant of ragtime and the blues. Like the blues, ragtime emerged from the traditional Black-American folk music of the nineteenth century. Ragtime's inventors are thought to be travelling minstrels who combined elements of Euro-American folk dance and fiddle music with syncopated African rhythms to create a new distinctive musical genre. Ragtime music was characterized by a syncopated melody played with a steady, marchlike harmony part.

Jazz first became popular in the New Orleans area at the turn of the century. This early jazz is often termed *New Orleans jazz*. Like the blues, once jazz spread to other urban centers around the country, it took on new forms. Dixieland and Harlem style jazz added some sophistication to the basic sound—and explored the potential of different instruments in the jazz band. In the 1920s, jazz entered the mainstream of popular song and made its debut on the Broadway stage. Since jazz is largely an instrumental form, musicians found that many older songs could be "jazzed up" to enjoy successful revivals. If a song got played enough by jazz musicians, it became known as a *jazz standard*.

Through the years, jazz has claimed many popular songs, folk tunes, and blues songs for its own. These jazz standards include traditional songs like "A-Tisket A-Tasket" and "Frankie and Johnny," as well as commercial hits like "Tea for Two" and "Alexander's Ragtime Band." In fact, most of the songs written by jazz-influenced composers such as Irving Berlin, George Gershwin, and Jerome Kern were reinterpreted by jazz musicians as standard pieces in their performance repertoire.

The Entertainer

In 1973, Marvin Hamlisch adapted compositions of Scott Joplin to create the score for the Academy Award–winning film *The Sting*. Joplin's ragtime classic, "The Entertainer," served as the theme song for the movie—and became a gold-record hit for Hamlisch in 1974. The popular movie soundtrack and hit single created a renewed public interest in ragtime music—and made Scott Joplin's name a household word for the 1970s and beyond.

Here, you will get a chance to sharpen your tablature and music-reading skills as you play the syncopated melody to "The Entertainer." The best way to play a single-line melody like this is with a pick, using downstrokes for notes which fall on the beats and upstrokes for notes on the offbeats.

If you want to play "The Entertainer" with your fingers, you will find suggested right-hand fingerings for the tricky spots. In general, just make sure that you are alternating fingers—never play two eighth-notes in a row with the same finger. It may help your learning the piece to write in your own fingerings.

The Entertainer

A-Tisket A-Tasket

Ella Fitzgerald is perhaps the greatest jazz singer of all time. After winning the Harlem Amateur Hour in 1934, she created a popular sensation with her jazzy rendition of "A-Tisket, A-Tasket."

In this arrangement, you will get a chance to learn some new jazz chords as well as some new strumming techniques. (Jazz guitarists call this type of chord backup *comping*.) The Gmaj7 chord is the same one used in "Aura Lee," and the Am7 is the same form as the Gm7 used in that song except that you play it at the fifth fret instead of the third. The change from Gmaj7 to G6 is a tough one, but concentrate on using your fourth finger as a pivot finger. The D9 chord has the same type of third-finger bar as the Am7, only here it covers the top three strings. The G_9^6 features bars with both the first and third fingers.

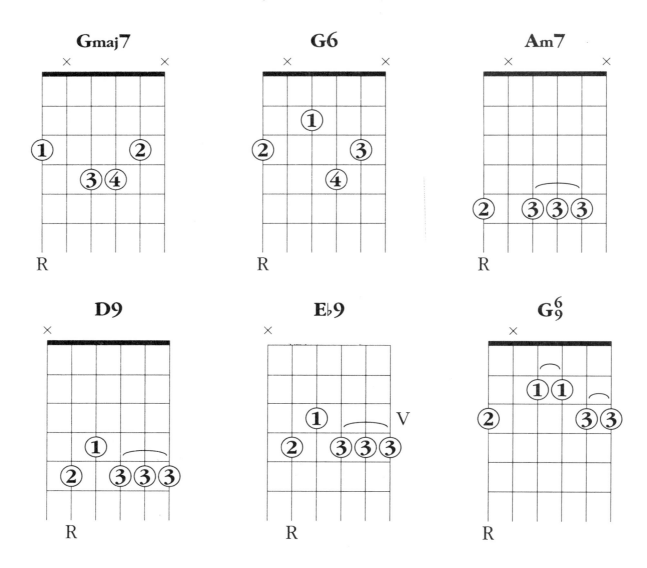

The best way to learn these new chords is to practice the song—isolate the changes that give you trouble and play them over and over until they become second nature. Once you get the hang of the syncopated strumming patterns as notated, try coming up with your own variations.

A-Tisket A-Tasket

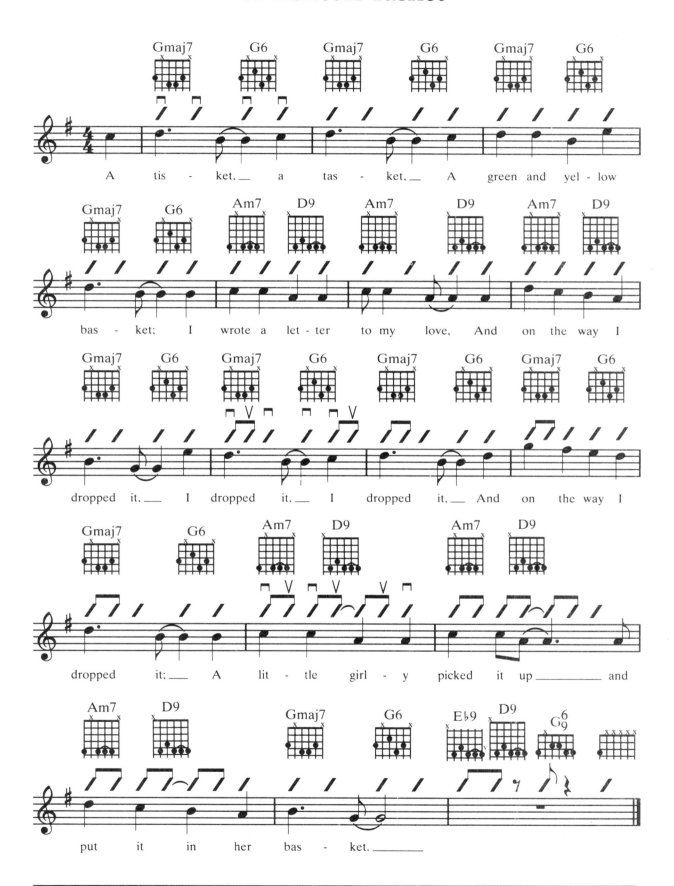

Classical

Technically speaking, classical music is any serious music composed between 1750 and 1820. This term is also commonly applied to music of a serious nature composed in any period—from the late Renaissance to the present. There is a rich literature of music for classical guitar that includes pieces written for guitar, lute, and other guitarlike instruments, as well as transcriptions of music written for all different instruments throughout the ages. Considering the influence of classical guitar music and technique on modern rock, heavy metal, and jazz guitarists, it is a good idea to have a bit of classical background no matter what style you want to play.

Classical guitarists never use picks, but they do grow the nails on their right-hand thumbs and fingers. If you play fingerstyle a lot, you may want to consider letting your fingernails grow until you can just see them peeking over the tops of your fingertips when you look at your hand palm-up. If you do, be sure to file each nail so that it is rounded and smooth. You already have learned a smattering of classical technique in this book when you studied rest strokes, free strokes, and other fingerpicking techniques. Get ready to apply what you know to two mainstays of the beginner's classical repertoire.

Estudio

This *estudio,* or "study," was written by the famous guitar teacher and composer Dionisio Aguado (1784–1849) to help his students learn the kind of right-hand coordination they would need to become good classical guitarists. As you play this simple study, you should notice that it is very much like the fingerpicking pieces you have learned. The main difference is that in a classical piece you tend to think less in terms of chords and more in terms of melody. In "Estudio," there are really two melodies: The main one consists of the notes played by the thumb; while the index and middle fingers play a countermelody. Keep this in mind when you play the piece, and try to make the thumb melody really sing. Although many of the left-hand positions are similar to chords you know, you will notice that fingerings are sometimes altered to allow you to get from one position to another easily. This will help you to play the melody and countermelody in a smooth and connected manner.

There are several *dynamic markings* in "Estudio" which tell you when to play louder or softer:
- At the beginning, the symbol *mp* tells you to start off playing *mezzo piano,* which means "medium soft."
- In measures 5 and 6, the *crescendo symbol* (<) tells you to get gradually louder, so that by measure 7, you are playing *mezzo forte,* or "medium loud," as indicated by the symbol *mf.*
- Throughout measures 7 and 8, the *descrescendo symbol* (>) calls for softer and softer playing, so that the last half note in measure 8 is played *piano,* "soft," as indicated by the symbol *p.*

There are two important *tempo markings* in "Estudio" which call for changes in playing speed.
- The word *ritard* in measure 16 means "slow down."
- In the next measure, *a tempo* tells you to resume the previous speed.

Play this lovely classical piece now at a slow and steady tempo.

Estudio

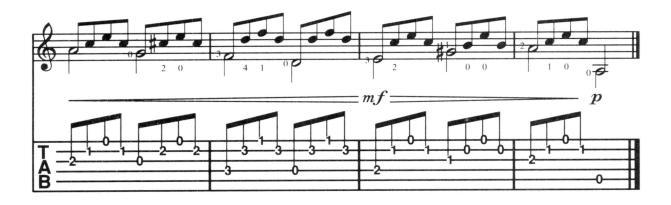

Romanze

While often attributed to the renowned guitarist and composer Francisco Tárrega (1852–1909), this "Romanze" is more likely a traditional Spanish folktune. It is certainly among the best-loved gems in the standard classical guitar repertoire.

You will need to use all three right-hand fingers for this one. In the repeating pattern of *a-m-i* triplets, the notes played by the ring finger make up the melody—try playing them with rest strokes. (Notice that it is not necessary to mark the triplets after the first couple of measures.) Since this piece moves all over neck, and there are no chord forms per se for long stretches at a time, it is difficult to find pivot fingers to help you out with all of the position changes. Work on arriving at each new position by leading with the finger that frets the melody note.

The very last chord in "Romanze" is played in *harmonics,* as indicated by the diamond shaped notes. To produce these bell-like tones, lightly lay your left-hand third finger across the top three strings, directly over the twelfth fret. As soon as you pluck the strings, remove your third finger to allow the harmonics to ring out. You will hear the same notes as the open strings would produce one octave higher.

There are no easy ways to play some of the difficult finger stretches in this piece—notably the one on the B chord at the beginning of measure 11. Just take heart that it is possible for anyone to do, keep your wrist low and your left elbow close to your body, and remember the magic word: *Practice.*

Romanze

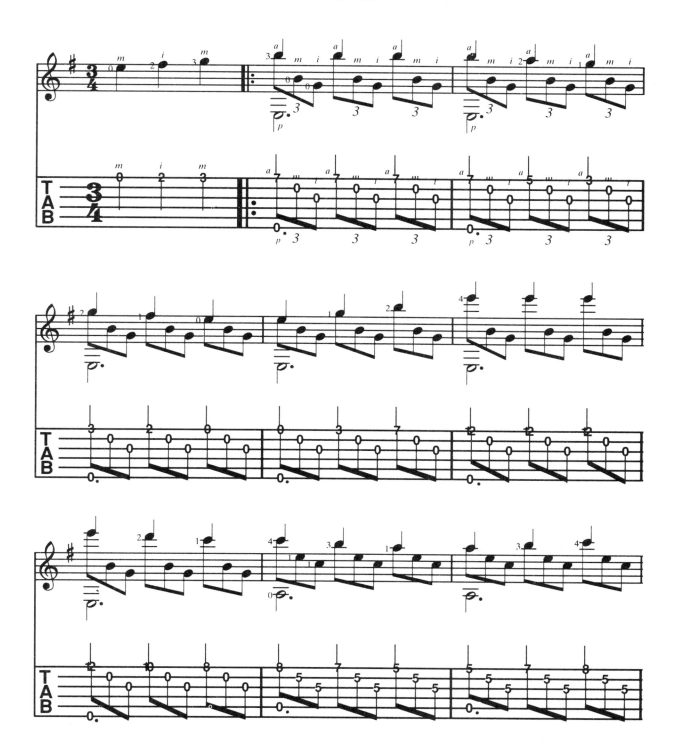

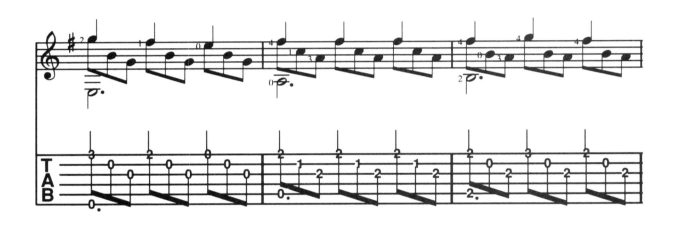

Further Study

Congratulations! You have completed a comprehensive course in guitar that will provide a broad foundation for your continued development and personal playing style. The "Table of Notes" and "Table of Chords" which follow will provide you with the key to hours of further study. Use these to explore reading and playing the chords and melody of your favorite songs, as well as ones that are unfamiliar to you. You'll find hours of enjoyment reading through sheet music and song collections as you strengthen these important reading skills.

You may also wish to pursue an in-depth study of chord forms and structure, as is provided in any good music-theory textbook. This further study is especially advisable for those who wish to compose or arrange music. A basic understanding of the more advanced theoretical aspects of written music can only serve to enhance your guitar playing abilities. (Naturally, a well-recommended guitar teacher would also greatly enhance your self-study program.) However, at this point, you have all the facts you need to continue your development as a knowledgable and competent guitarist—and the music store and music library will provide you with many new doorways to a lifetime of playing enjoyment.

Table of Notes

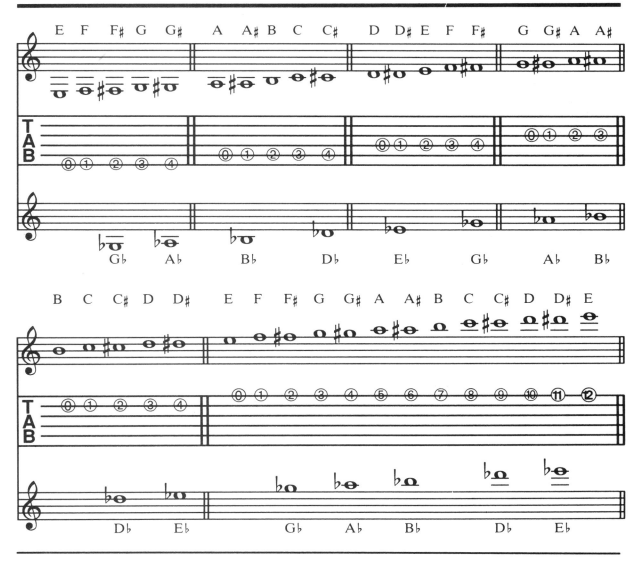

Table of Chords

This table includes basic chords in root position and some common forms of moveable chords. Remember that a moveable chord form may be moved up or down on the neck, and the name of the chord will be determined by the root of the chord (indicated in the diagrams by an **R**).

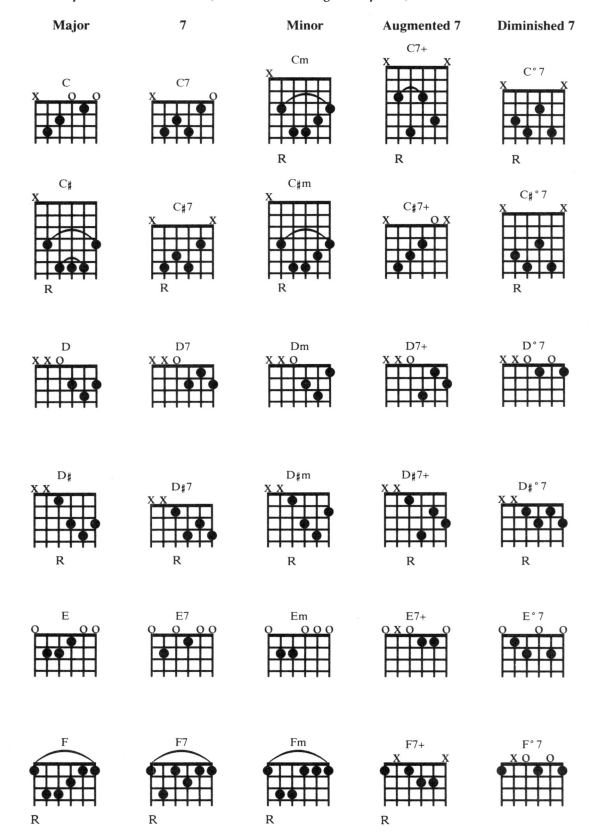

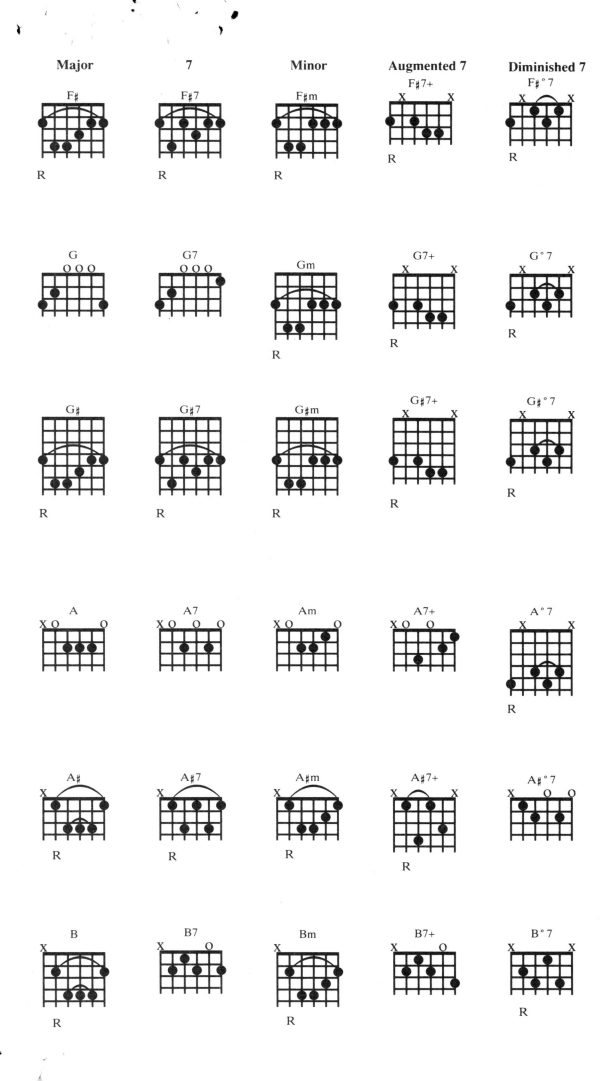